AMERICA FIRST AGENDA

TEN PILLARS FOR RESTORING
A NATION UNDER GOD!

The America First Policy Institute (AFPI) is a 501(c)(3) non-profit, non-partisan research institute.

AFPI exists to advance policies that put the American people first. Our guiding principles are liberty, free enterprise, national greatness, American military superiority, foreign policy engagement in the American interest, and the primacy of American workers, families, and communities in all we do.

americafirstpolicy.com

America First Agenda: Ten Pillars for Restoring a Nation Under God

Copyright © 2024 America First Policy Institute

All rights reserved. No part of this booklet may be reproduced or transmitted in any form or by any means, electronic or mechanical, including photocopying, recording, or by any information storage and retrieval system, without permission in writing from the publisher.

Printed in the United States of America.

Make the Greatest Economy in the World Work for All Americans

Put Patients and Doctors Back in Charge of Healthcare

Restore America's Historic Commitment to Freedom, Equality, and Self-Governance

Give Parents More Control Over Their Children's Education

Finish the Wall, End Human Trafficking,
and Defeat the Drug Cartels

Deliver Peace Through Strength

Make America Energy Independent

Make It Easy to Vote and Hard to Cheat

Provide Safe and Secure Communities So All Americans Can Live Their Lives in Peace

Fight Government Corruption by Draining the Swamp

Why Christians Must Engage Now... Before It's Too Late

For nearly 2,000 years, the gospel of Jesus Christ has been the greatest force for human flourishing the planet has ever seen. Yes, the good news has redeemed countless lost individuals and swept them into an eternity in heaven. But the effects here—in this broken world—have been profound as well.

Without a Christian worldview and values, Western civilization—and the extraordinary progress, prosperity, freedom, and equality it has produced—does not emerge. And the fullest expression of that civilization has been the United States of America—a nation founded by people rooted in biblical truth who crafted a constitutional republic unlike anything the world had ever seen.

WE'VE LOST OUR WAY

But no one has to tell you that America has lost its way. You see it everywhere you look. You see long-cherished freedoms—bought with blood and sacrifice by successive generations—eroding rapidly. The values that produced unprecedented order, opportunity, and prosperity are mocked and discarded, producing these consequences:

- Rising consumer prices since the start of the Biden Administration. Prices have risen 17% since the start of the Biden Administration—that's the largest increase in consumer prices during a president's first term since the 1980s.
- Growing lawlessness at our border and in our once-great cities.
- Diminishing confidence in the integrity of our electoral systems, governing institutions, and foreign policy.
- Increasing radical agendas that seek to indoctrinate children.

THE WAY BACK

Yet, it is not too late. IF...if a saving remnant comprised of people of faith will awaken, God's people can turn the tide. This will require the power of prayer and engagement in the public square.

To this end, the America First Policy Institute (AFPI) has established 10 policy pillars, presented in detail in the *America First Agenda: Guide to the Issues* and designed to serve all Americans.

America First Agenda: Ten Pillars for Restoring a Nation Under God interprets the policy objectives of the America First Agenda through the lens of their biblical foundations and applications to provide Christians with more information on the issues and solutions needed to restore our Nation that was founded on Judeo-Christian principles.

PURPOSE OF THE BIBLICAL FOUNDATIONS PROJECT

The idea of mixing religion and public discourse has been made into an untouchable idea in the United States, but in reality, God has called His Church to be active in the issues of our day. This project will underline the biblical foundation for each of AFPI's 10 foundational pillars for America. Without the guidance of the Holy Bible in a world full of evil, it is impossible to safeguard the future of America for the next generation. Our Christian and biblical values over the last two centuries matter. The extraordinary progress, prosperity, freedom, and equality it has produced matter. The Church in the United States must play a central role in standing for the values and freedoms that have made America the most prosperous nation on Earth. The purpose is not to build a state religion but to maintain the foundational Judeo-Christian values that have secured our Nation's future over the last two and half centuries.

Jesus has called His Church to participate in the marketplace of ideas according to His gospel. We are called to be the light of the world and the salt of the Earth. If the Church does not engage in the issues of the day, it is missing a historic opportunity at a critical point in America's story to bring the Kingdom of Heaven to Earth. We must act. We must vote. We must run for public office. We must plant Jesus in every space while we are still allowed to stand and speak God's truth.

As we have seen in history, in the words of Lord Acton, "power tends to corrupt, and absolute power corrupts absolutely." We are witnessing the progression of that adage every day in our government, our media, and our schools. Freedoms and liberties guaranteed in our Constitution are under assault. This fight is not just about the culture of America; it's about the Kingdom of God and the Church's divine mission to be salt and light in an era of increasing darkness.

It is not too late for America. And it is not too late to surrender to the unshakable truth found in 2 Chronicles 7:14: "If My people who are called by My name will humble themselves, and pray and seek My face, and turn from their wicked ways, then I will hear from heaven, and will forgive their sin and heal their land." This is a call to action for God's people. Prayer is the first step, but it must be coupled with action. The book of James declares that "faith without works is dead." Faith in action can produce lasting policy that honors God and His design for mankind through righteous governance. **In other words, America is a country under God, indivisible, that delivers liberty and justice for all.**

The Biblical Foundations Project aims to equip pastors, churches, and all people of faith in America with language that will empower them to speak to the core issues challenging America's future. The goal is to inspire people to articulate why America First policies are not only the right direction for the American people but also how they are grounded in the eternal truth of Scripture.

To restore America to a Nation under God, the Church must pray and act.

For more information and to stay up to date on the Biblical Foundations Project, please see below.

1. **TEXT *FAITH* TO *70107***
TO SIGN UP FOR REGULAR UPDATES.

2. **SCAN QR CODE >**
TO VISIT OUR WEBSITE.

KEY CONCEPT:
Faith and Politics DO Mix in America

"Politics matters because policy matters; policy matters because people matter." - Pastor Paula White-Cain

Throughout the Bible, God has used His people in various aspects of governance to be a light for Him in this world. From Joseph to Moses to Daniel to Esther and even to Jesus and Paul in the New Testament, God has used His people to influence the governments of the day for His divine purpose. Today is no different. The Church is God's force for good in the world and the United States, and this force does not end where government begins. The Church is to go into all the world, not just areas where it is considered politically correct. This is the mission of the Church.

This booklet is designed for pastors, ministry leaders, and other like-minded community leaders who wish to utilize the content of this project to advance an agenda that will save America. Below is a list of items that outline the biblical mandate for the Church to engage in public discourse drawn from an introductory sermon series developed by the America First Policy Institute.

- God has always cared about governance and calls His Church to be His influence in these systems.
- The Bible has a lot to say about government in both the Old and New Testaments. God has used people in government throughout the history of the world.
- The words "politics" and "religion" have been twisted over the years to be something they are not. They have been separated, but they belong together.
- We are ultimately citizens of heaven, and the calling of Christians is to be representatives of Christ—the salt and light—on Earth and in all aspects of life on Earth.
- America was founded as a self-governing nation on biblical principles. The Ten Commandments and Christian teachings have been the foundation that created the American legal system.
- Self-governance is a biblical concept that has three main components: the rule of law, consent of the governed, and private property.

The Calling from God
God has called His Church to be a part of political discourse and the system of governance. Jesus called His Church the salt of the Earth and the light to the world. This salt and light do not end where government begins.

God's Idea
Good governance is God's idea. Mankind cannot have good governance without the foundational principles of God's design for self-governance — the rule of law, private property, and dispersed decision-making with the consent of the governed.

The Church & Government
Worldly philosophy, like Marxism, influences American politics and attempts to redefine the relationship that the Church has with government. The religious nature of Marxism places man at the top and removes God completely.

America's Core
America was founded on Judeo-Christian principles by people who escaped totalitarianism and tyranny from unjust and wrongful governance. They founded a country with the understanding that power corrupts and absolute power corrupts absolutely. This is why Christian principles are at the core of America.

Policy + Jesus
The Bible makes it clear that religion and good policy mix well. In fact, the best policy is grounded in the teachings of Jesus and the Bible.

Designed for Good Governance
Having Christian values as the foundation of a country sets the people in line with God's perfect design for good governance.

FOUNDATIONAL UNDERSTANDING:
The Structure of the United States Government

"For the LORD is our judge, the LORD is our lawgiver, the LORD is our king; it is he who will save us." – Isaiah 33:22 (NIV)

The U.S. government has three branches that preside over the affairs of the nation. The executive, judicial, and legislative branches all conduct specific tasks outlined in the Constitution of the United States. The government carries immense power over the lives of its citizens and the welfare of society overall.

The executive branch is led by the president of the United States and his or her cabinet. This includes the vice president and 15 secretaries that preside over the various departments, such as the Department of State and Department of Education. The cabinet has grown immensely since the founding of the United States when it contained only three secretaries. Overall, more than 4 million Americans—civilian and military—work for the federal government.

The judicial branch is responsible for deciding the constitutionality of laws and resolving disputes about federal laws. This includes the United States Supreme Court, which consists of nine judges appointed by the president and confirmed by the Senate. The appointment of a U.S. Supreme Court justice is a life-long appointment. This makes it critical in the long-term legal structure of the country and in safeguarding the rights and freedoms of the people from the overreach of the extensive government bureaucracy.

The legislative branch is the Congress of the United States, which includes the House of Representatives and the Senate, both elected by the people. The Senate has 100 senators (two from each state), and the House of Representatives has 435 members. The number of representatives for each state is determined by the population of the state. A more populated state like California has 53 representatives, while a less populated state like South Dakota has only one. However, every state has two senators, balancing power and allowing for equal representation across the nation.

The United States government was masterfully designed by the founding fathers with a clear goal in mind—separation of powers. This design ensures that no single branch has ultimate power over another and that a strong system of checks and balances is in place. Self-governance is at the core of the system, where the people have the ultimate say in how our Nation should be governed. This is clearly stated in our founding documents with the phrase, "*We the People...*"

The following pages include AFPI's biblically based analysis of each of the 10 pillars that guide AFPI's broader policy work. The material provides a deeper understanding of why these pillars are the right direction for America because they are grounded in facts, current polling, and policy solutions. More importantly, it shows that the pillars are rooted in key Scriptures that are critical to restoring one nation under God.

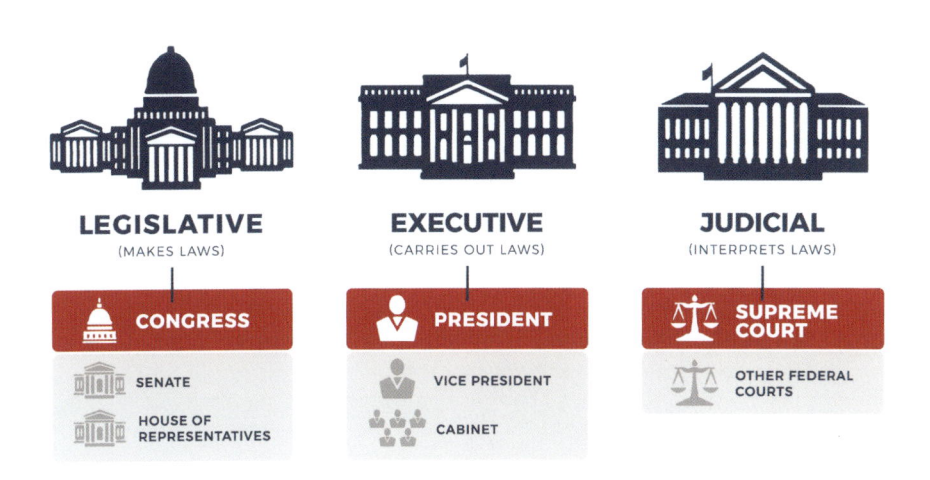

LEGISLATIVE
(MAKES LAWS)

- **CONGRESS**
  - SENATE
  - HOUSE OF REPRESENTATIVES

EXECUTIVE
(CARRIES OUT LAWS)

- **PRESIDENT**
  - VICE PRESIDENT
  - CABINET

JUDICIAL
(INTERPRETS LAWS)

- **SUPREME COURT**
  - OTHER FEDERAL COURTS

Make the Greatest Economy in the World Work for All Americans

From beginning to end, the Scriptures recognize the value of work and that people should be free to enjoy the fruits of their hard work. From the Garden of Eden to the Promised Land to the stewardship parables of Jesus, we see the Bible commanding, encouraging, and codifying this principle. At the same time, the Bible consistently warns against the destructive force of envy, coveting, theft, and the unjust use of power. A government should be driven by policies that foster a country's creativity and economic power and that support the individual dignity of workers rather than policies that stifle the autonomy of individuals to provide for their families.

When one looks at our country today, the sense of fear about the future of the economy is palpable. One sees waves of Marxism and Socialism infiltrating society and threats of central bank digital currencies looming. Once prominent cities are beginning to resemble poverty-stricken, third-world countries. In response, many politicians offer a singular solution of raising taxes and spending more on failing programs that cost taxpayers more hard-earned money. While inflation soars and prices increase, more and more Americans are feeling the pain of failed leftist policies. The U.S. government now spends money faster than the speed of light and often without regard to the will of the people. This neglect of the American people jeopardizes the prosperity and sustainability of future generations.

When a government robs its citizens of freedom... when it attacks hardworking Americans with crippling taxation to further empower and enrich the corrupt and powerful... when it crushes the poor and middle-class families through inflationary policies... when it punishes initiative and hard work while rewarding vice... when it gathers to itself the power to pick winners and losers in our economy instead of allowing the market to run its course, it destroys common prosperity and fosters tyranny.

Yes, the care of orphans, widows, and the poor is near and dear to God's heart. It is, therefore, solely the assignment of God's people—the Church—to give voluntarily and joyfully, not "under compulsion," as Paul says in 2 Corinthians 9:7.

The America First Agenda seeks to champion policies that will rebuild our great American economy and restore hope and prosperity for all Americans. It puts the prosperity of American citizens first, restores and strengthens the American free enterprise system, defends workers and entrepreneurs, promotes growth that uplifts forgotten communities, and celebrates the innovative spirit of the American people. We recognize that our Nation's economic prosperity reached unprecedented heights through Americans' grit, ingenuity, and innovative spirit. When America First economic policies are followed, the opportunities for America to soar to new heights are boundless.

KEY SCRIPTURES

"Remember the LORD your God, for it is He who gives you the ability to produce wealth..."
Deuteronomy 8:18 (NIV)

"When you eat the fruit of the labor of your hands, you will be happy and it will go well for you."
Psalm 128:2 (NASB)

"Let no debt remain outstanding, except the continuing debt to love one another, for whoever loves others has fulfilled the law."
Romans 13:8 (NIV)

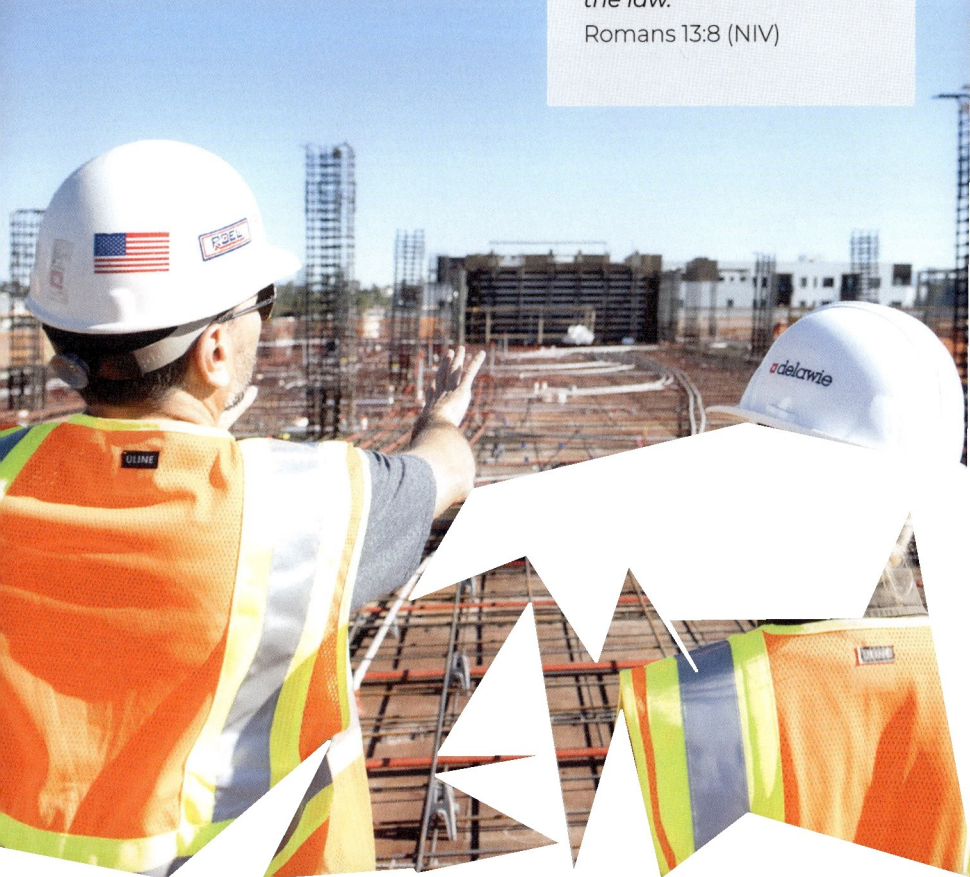

THE AMERICA FIRST AGENDA

- End Historic Out-of-Control Inflation
- Fight for American Workers and Their Wages
- Negotiate Trade Deals that Protect American Workers and Consumers and Protect our National Security
- Make the Tax Cuts and Jobs Act Permanent
- Build Supply Chains that Rely on American Workers and our Allies
- Build the World's Greatest Infrastructure System
- Enhance Opportunity Zones to Strengthen America's Forgotten Communities

Public Opinion

Below is a list of recent polling data that highlights what the American people think about these issues.

From Scott Rasmussen National Surveys

88% OF VOTERS **FAVOR MAKING THE GREATEST ECONOMY IN THE WORLD** WORK FOR ALL AMERICANS (June 2022).

64% OF VOTERS **RATE THEIR PERSONAL FINANCES AS FAIR OR POOR** (September 2023).

64% OF VOTERS SAY THEIR **INCOME HAS BEEN FALLING BEHIND WITH INFLATION** (August 2023).

57% OF VOTERS SAY THAT THE ECONOMY IS GETTING EITHER **SOMEWHAT WORSE OR MUCH WORSE** (September 2023).

45% OF VOTERS RATE THE U.S. *ECONOMY AS POOR* (September 2023).

41% OF VOTERS CONSIDER THE *ECONOMY AND INFLATION TO BE THE MOST IMPORTANT ISSUES* FACING THE COUNTRY RIGHT NOW (September 2023).

Only 37% OF VOTERS SAY THEY ARE *BETTER OFF TODAY THAN THEY WERE FOUR YEARS AGO* (August 2023).

44% OF VOTERS SAY THE *UNITED STATES IS IN A RECESSION* (September 2023).

75% OF VOTERS SAY THAT TAXES IN THE UNITED STATES ARE *SOMEWHAT OR MUCH TOO HIGH* (May 2023).

90% OF VOTERS SAY THEY ARE *PAYING THEIR FAIR SHARE OR MORE THAN THEIR FAIR SHARE IN TAXES* (May 2023).

54% OF VOTERS SAY PASSING A BUDGET THAT INCREASES TAXES ON MOST AMERICANS *WOULD BE WORSE FOR AMERICA THAN A PARTIAL GOVERNMENT SHUTDOWN* (September 2023).

Deep Dive into the Issues

These facts are shaping the reality for everyday Americans, which is why they undergird the motivation for AFPI's commitment to advance policies that put the American people first.

End Historic Out-of-Control Inflation.
Under the Biden Administration:
- Prices have risen 17% overall.
- Gas prices are up more than 50%.
- Interest rates are the highest in 22 years.
- 61% of Americans are living paycheck to paycheck.

Fight for American Workers and Their Wages.
- Workers saw record-high median income gains, 50-year lows for unemployment, and record-low poverty for all demographic groups during the previous administration before the arrival of the COVID-19 pandemic.
- Since the current administration took office, paychecks are down 3%.
- The share of jobs with government occupational license requirements has risen from 5% in the 1950s to 25-30% today, accounting for 2.85 million lost jobs and $200 billion in higher prices.

Negotiate Trade Deals that Protect American Workers and Consumers and Protect our National Security.
- The U.S. trade deficit with the world grew to more than $1 trillion in 2021, more than doubling on an annual basis over the past two decades. This decades-long trend of increasing deficits cumulatively represents a transfer of trillions of dollars of American wealth to other countries, with a large share going to China.
- More than 60,000 American factories were shut down in the decades following the implementation of the *North American Free Trade Agreement* (NAFTA) in 1994 and China's accession to the World Trade Organization in 2001. At the same time, America lost one in four manufacturing jobs, with research finding a strong link between these losses and the normalization of trade relations with China.
- China's intellectual property theft is estimated to cost America anywhere from $225 to $600 billion annually in counterfeit goods, pirated software, and stolen trade secrets.
- About 15,000 manufacturing jobs were lost in 2016, while the American economy gained nearly 500,000 such jobs from 2017 to 2020.

Make the Tax Cuts and Jobs Act Permanent.
- Under the act, unemployment fell to a 50-year low of 3.5% in February 2020, and more jobs were available than individuals unemployed. The act was signed on December 22, 2017.
- The female unemployment rate hit its lowest rate in nearly 70 years before

the pandemic.
- Incomes soared by $5,000 between 2017 and 2019, with income growth setting an all-time record in 2019.
- American households in the bottom 50% of the socioeconomic scale saw a 40% increase in their real net worth, while wages grew fastest for low-income and blue-collar workers.
- The U.S. experienced fast, non-inflationary growth, with inflation rising less than 2% in 2019, defying many forecasters' expectations.
- Key provisions of the successful Tax Cuts and Jobs Act are set to expire by December 31, 2025, if Congress does not take action to make the provisions permanent.

Build Supply Chains that Rely Only on American Workers and Our Allies.
- About 55% of S&P 500 companies cited the supply chain as a negative factor in their first-quarter earnings this year.
- Heightened goods consumption arising during the pandemic resulted in the U.S. trade deficit for goods surpassing $1 trillion for the first time in 2021—an increase of 21% over 2020. This increased the reliance of our supply chain on overseas producers.
- The current U.S. trade deficit for goods is $948.1 billion.

Build the World's Greatest Infrastructure System.
- Of the 617,000 bridges in the U.S., 12% are at least 80 years old.
- As many as 36% of U.S. bridges need major repair work or should be replaced.
- At the current administration's pace, repairing these bridges would take 30 years.
- The inflation-adjusted cost per mile of interstate construction is more than three times what it was in the 1960s, causing each infrastructure dollar not to go as far.

Enhance Opportunity Zones (OZs) to Strengthen America's Forgotten Communities.
- As many as 32 million Americans live in the 8,829 economically distressed areas designated as OZs—a program established by the 2017 Tax Cuts and Jobs Act.
- As many as 28.9% of the population in economically disadvantaged OZs live in poverty.
- Areas receiving an OZ designation are expected to gain $11 billion in new wealth through increased property values because of the OZ designation.
- An estimated one million people could be lifted out of poverty through investment brought by the OZ incentives.
- More than 1.2 million jobs are expected to be created because of the OZ designation.

Learn more at: agenda.americafirstpolicy.com/pillar/economy

2 Put Patients and Doctors Back in Charge of Healthcare

The Bible declares that we are fearfully and wonderfully made in the image of our Creator. We were knit together in our mothers' wombs—created for great works in Him. Ephesians 2:10 declares: "For we are God's masterpiece. He has created us anew in Christ Jesus, so we can do the good things he planned for us long ago." This divine design is at all levels of our lives, including our bodies and our health.

The responsibility to steward our bodies and health as individuals and as families is a foundational assumption in Scripture and vital to a free people. But bit by bit, our government in recent years has moved both responsibility and decision-making power out of the hands of families and their physicians and into the hands of faceless bureaucrats. This is the realization of Marxist and Socialist ideology in our healthcare—where mandates are placed on citizens and conscience protections for doctors are not honored. These radical principles usurp individual responsibility and authority and replace it with the requirements of the dominant ideology.

Today, the high costs, limited choices, and variable quality of healthcare in the country are significant concerns for Americans. This not only affects the long-term welfare of individuals but of the country.

Currently, there are many in places of power who manipulate healthcare to benefit well-connected firms and special interests, all while expanding the power and size of government bureaucracies. This does not fulfill the core mission of the healthcare system—to improve the health of ALL Americans so they can best fulfill their God-given purpose.

True self-governance includes the notion that "We the People" have autonomy over our health and, ultimately, the critical decisions that determine our overall well-being. The America First Agenda seeks to put patients and doctors back in charge of healthcare. The goal is to unleash human creativity to co-labor with God for health solutions and to provide transparency that gives Americans the agency to best steward their health.

KEY SCRIPTURES

"Or do you not know that your body is the temple of the Holy Spirit who is in you, whom you have from God, and you are not your own?"
1 Corinthians 6:19 (NASB)

"Learn to do good; seek justice, rebuke the oppressor; defend the fatherless, plead for the widow."
Isaiah 1:17 (NKJV)

"Beloved, I pray that you may prosper in all things and be in health, just as your soul prospers."
3 John 1:2 (NKJV)

"For we are God's masterpiece. He has created us anew in Christ Jesus, so we can do the good things he planned for us long ago."
Ephesians 2:10 (NLT)

THE **AMERICA FIRST** AGENDA | 19

THE AMERICA FIRST AGENDA

★ Enhance Access to Trusted Doctors and Appropriate Care

★ Protect the Most Vulnerable, Including Seniors and People with Preexisting Conditions

★ Increase Affordable Health Plans and Alternative Forms of Coverage

★ Promote Individual Control of Healthcare

★ Lower Prescription Drug Prices

★ Promote Transparent, Upfront Pricing

Public Opinion

Below is a list of recent polling data that highlights what the American people think about these issues.

From Scott Rasmussen National Surveys

86% OF VOTERS **FAVOR PUTTING PATIENTS AND DOCTORS BACK IN CHARGE OF OUR HEALTHCARE SYSTEM** (June 2022).

ONLY 9% OF VOTERS RATE THE OVERALL U.S. **HEALTHCARE SYSTEM AS EXCELLENT** (April 2022).

ONLY 27% OF VOTERS **RATE THE QUALITY OF HEALTHCARE THEY PERSONALLY RECEIVE AS EXCELLENT** (July 2022).

74% OF VOTERS SAY GIVING INDIVIDUALS *MORE CONTROL OVER THEIR OWN HEALTHCARE DECISIONS WOULD MAKE OUR HEALTHCARE SYSTEM BETTER* (April 2022).

64% OF VOTERS *STRONGLY FAVOR A PLAN TO ENSURE PATIENTS ARE TREATED EQUALLY,* FAIRLY, AND WITH RESPECT (July 2022).

61% OF VOTERS *STRONGLY FAVOR A PLAN TO IMPROVE THE OVERALL HEALTH* OF THE AMERICAN PEOPLE (July 2022).

62% OF VOTERS *STRONGLY FAVOR A PLAN THAT ALLOWS THEM TO RECEIVE PERSONALIZED CARE AND COVERAGE* THAT WORKS BEST FOR THEM (July 2022).

77% OF VOTERS SAY REQUIRING HEALTHCARE PROVIDERS TO *DISCLOSE ALL COSTS BEFORE PROVIDING SERVICES WOULD MAKE OUR HEALTHCARE SYSTEM BETTER* (April 2022).

80% OF VOTERS SAY INDIVIDUAL AMERICANS *SHOULD BE ALLOWED TO PURCHASE ANY HEALTH INSURANCE* PRODUCT APPROVED BY THEIR STATE'S HEALTH INSURANCE COMMISSIONER (April 2022).

ONLY 33% OF VOTERS BELIEVE THAT HAVING THE *FEDERAL GOVERNMENT TAKE OVER THE HEALTHCARE SYSTEM WOULD MAKE IT BETTER* (April 2022).

Deep Dive into the Issues

These facts are shaping the reality for everyday Americans, which is why they undergird the motivation for AFPI's commitment to advance policies that put the American people first.

Enhance Access to Trusted Doctors and Appropriate Care.
- Direct primary care has been associated with 20% lower employee premiums, 30% lower out-of-pocket costs, and a 40% reduction in emergency department visits.
- About 90% of the $4.1 trillion in annual health expenditures are used to treat people with chronic and mental health conditions. 60% of Americans have at least one chronic condition, and 42% have multiple chronic conditions.
- 5% of the population accounts for 50% of healthcare expenditures, and 50% of the population accounts for 97% of expenditures.
- Only 7% of U.S. adults ages 35 and older received all the high-priority, appropriate clinical preventive services in 2018, according to the most recent data available.

Protect the Most Vulnerable, Including Seniors and People with Preexisting Conditions.
- The Hospital Insurance Trust Fund, which pays for hospitals and post-acute services providers under Medicare Part A, will become insolvent in 2028.
- States that expanded Medicaid enrolled twice as many able-bodied adults as estimated, with per-person costs exceeding original estimates by 76%, leading to a combined cost overrun of 157%.
- Medicare Advantage outperforms traditional Medicare, including more preventive care services, fewer hospital admissions and emergency department visits, shorter hospital and skilled nursing facility lengths-of-stay, and lower healthcare spending.

Increase Affordable Health Plans and Alternative Forms of Coverage.
- Average family premiums increased 47%, from $15,073 in 2011 to $22,221 in 2021, after the passage of the Affordable Care Act (ACA). In the same period, average general deductibles for single coverage increased by 92%, from $747 to $1,434.
- Three-quarters of the United States health insurance market is highly concentrated.
- Premiums for small businesses nearly doubled from 2003 to 2018, from a total cost of $9,321 for family coverage per worker to $18,296. From 2003 to 2018, 31% fewer small businesses offered coverage.
- Short-term, limited-duration plan premiums typically cost significantly less than premiums for individual plans bought on the Obamacare exchanges—sometimes almost half the cost.

Promote Individual Control of Healthcare.
- The ACA created a tax penalty for Americans without health insurance. From tax years 2014 through 2017, 24.4 million tax returns showed individual mandate penalties amounting to $11.97 billion.
- The ACA's employer mandate is a greater burden to smaller firms, as costs are about one-third more per worker than the costs for firms with more than 10,000 workers.
- About 250,000 jobs were eliminated by businesses nationwide to avoid being subject to the ACA's employer mandate.
- 31 million Americans currently have HSAs. Of the $1 trillion in employer-sponsored health insurance premiums in 2021, only a small portion of that amount—$39 billion, or 4%—was contributed to HSAs.
- The Trump Administration's health reimbursement arrangement rules are projected to be used by 800,000 employers and to decrease the number of uninsured individuals by 800,000 by 2029.

Lower Prescription Drug Prices.
- 90% of filled prescriptions are for generic drugs, which are generally cheaper. Generics account for only 18% of prescription drug spending.
- As evidence of increased foreign "free-riding," European countries paid 32% of United States prices in 2017, compared to 51% of United States prices in 2003 for many high-sales volume pharmaceutical drugs.
- From 2017 to 2019, the FDA approved record-breaking numbers of generic drugs that contributed to the 2.4% annual price decrease in 2019—the largest in nearly 50 years.

Promote Transparent, Upfront Pricing.
- In 2022, a record-high 38% of adults reported that they or a family member put off any sort of medical treatment during the past year due to costs—a 12-point rise from 26% in 2021.
- Prices for the same medical service can vary greatly by hospital. For example, routine colonoscopies can range from $148 to $15,789 in just the Dallas area.
- Only 36% of 2,000 surveyed hospitals in the United States were compliant with the CMS Hospital Price Transparency Rule as of July 2023.

Learn more at: agenda.americafirstpolicy.com/pillar/healthcare

Restore America's Historic Commitment to Freedom, Equality, and Self-Governance

We were created to be free. Freedom under God's rule—with individuals and families practicing "self-governance"—was His original, good plan for mankind. America's founders understood this. As a nation, we were born of a passion for liberty and the conviction that fundamental "unalienable rights" are granted by our Creator, not the government. The founders also understood that mankind is fallen and broken; therefore, power in the hands of fallen people would corrupt those who held it. The founders understood this better than most. The pilgrims crossed the Atlantic to flee their native England because they were persecuted for their beliefs. It was their desire for freedom that drove them to make the treacherous journey and begin a new life in a strange land. They understood that their rights did not come from the government but from God.

Unalienable rights cannot be removed either voluntarily or involuntarily. They are at the core of the human experience. Because God has given those rights to you, no entity on Earth can take them away. They are universal truths—true for every human being in the world. According to the U.S. Constitution, these rights include life, liberty, and the pursuit of happiness, and governments are instructed to secure these rights and not to take them away. The consent of the governed is what gives governments the power to secure the rights of the people.

However, the government today has moved at both state and federal levels to restrict people from these very rights. During the COVID-19 pandemic, churches were unjustly forced to shut their doors, and the overreach of the government seemed to have no bounds.

The same is true with the effects of political correctness. Americans feel compelled to self-censor and refrain from speaking their minds. Even the phrase "Merry Christmas" was labeled offensive by the extreme leftists who have, time after time, attacked traditional values under the guise of tolerance.

This is precisely why the founding fathers penned a Constitution brilliantly designed to restrict the reach and power of the government over individuals—including the Bill of Rights, which clearly spells out the rights and freedoms U.S. citizens enjoy.

Today, Christians are increasingly facing persecution, penalties, and sanctions for simply speaking their convictions and proclaiming the truths of the Bible. While forces are working to take down the freedoms Americans love and cherish, victories to advance freedoms continue to mount. Recent Supreme Court decisions in 303 *Creative LLC v. Elenis* and *Groff v. DeJoy* helped secure both religious freedom and freedom of speech for generations to come.

Furthermore, with the victory in the overturning of Roe v. Wade, the fight for life gained considerable ground that must continue to be defended in legislative bodies. Every victory for life must be celebrated and expanded to support women, families and babies. The United States does not need radical, extremist pro-abortion policy; it needs more support for mothers and babies and their families through wonderful organizations like Pregnancy Resource Centers. While the fight for life continues, so does the fight to ensure women have access to the necessary resources and opportunities.

Unfortunately, radical gender ideology has been infused into many aspects of society. It has usurped women's sports and wreaked havoc in the family, in many cases ripping away the rights of parents in the lives of their children. The radical left pushes this ideology on children through the schools, while parents are expected to accept what the government tells them. It's time to stand up for what is right for families and to restore the biblical truth that there are only two genders.

Equality, freedom, and self-governance were created by God. This includes religious freedom, a prime example of free will. From the Garden of Eden to the present day, mankind has possessed the freedom to choose God or not. This inherent, natural right was given to us by God, and no one else can take it away.

Mankind will choose how they live—either honoring God or not—but they have the right to make that decision. A core purpose of Christian engagement in these issues is to model freedom in Christ for ALL while standing for truth. The America First Agenda seeks to restore the innate value of each person by promoting freedom, equality, and self-governance.

KEY SCRIPTURES

"And He has made from one blood every nation of men to dwell on all the face of the earth, and has determined their preappointed times and the boundaries of their dwellings..."
Acts 17:26 (NKJV)

"The heart is deceitful above all things and desperately wicked; who can know it?"
Jeremiah 17:9 (KJV)

"Woe to those who enact unjust statutes, and to those who constantly record harmful decisions."
Isaiah 10:1 (NASB)

"For you, brethren, have been called to liberty; only do not use liberty as an opportunity for the flesh, but through love serve one another. For all the law is fulfilled in one word, even in this 'You shall love your neighbor as yourself.'"
Galatians 5:13-14 (NKJV)

"Live as people who are free not using your freedom as a cover-up for evil, but living as servants of God. Honor everyone. Love the brotherhood. Fear God. Honor the emperor."
1 Peter 2:16-17 (ESV)

THE AMERICA FIRST AGENDA

★ Defend our Constitutional Rights of Religious Liberty and Freedom of Conscience

★ Defend our Constitutional Right to Keep and Bear Arms

★ Stop Big Tech from Encroaching on Our Free Speech

★ Honor the Sanctity of Every Innocent Human Life

★ Defend Female Athletes and Preserve Fairness in Women's Sports

Public Opinion

Below is a list of recent polling data that highlights what the American people think about these issues.

From Scott Rasmussen National Surveys

85% OF VOTERS *FAVOR RESTORING AMERICA'S HISTORIC COMMITMENT* TO FREEDOM, EQUALITY, AND SELF-GOVERNANCE (June 2022).

77% OF VOTERS SAY THAT THE UNITED STATES WAS *FOUNDED ON THE IDEALS OF FREEDOM, EQUALITY, AND SELF-GOVERNANCE, BUT 61% OF VOTERS*, GENERALLY SPEAKING, *DO NOT BELIEVE THAT AMERICA IS DOING A BETTER JOB* AT LIVING UP TO THOSE IDEALS THAN IT DID IN EARLIER TIMES (August 2023).

42% OF VOTERS SAY THAT *ABORTION SHOULD BE ILLEGAL* IN ALL (7%) OR MOST (35%) CASES. AMONG THOSE WHO THINK IT SHOULD BE LEGAL IN AT LEAST SOME CASES, *75% BELIEVE THERE SHOULD BE AT LEAST SOME RESTRICTIONS* (September 2023).

58% OF VOTERS AGREE WITH THE FOLLOWING STATEMENT: *ABORTION IS A DIFFICULT ISSUE BECAUSE TWO LIVES ARE INVOLVED.* OUR GOAL SHOULD BE TO HELP WOMEN IN DIFFICULT SITUATIONS SO THAT THERE ARE FEWER ABORTIONS. ULTIMATELY, WE WOULD LIKE TO REACH A POINT WHERE ABORTION IS UNTHINKABLE (July 2023).

77% OF VOTERS *AGREE THAT SCIENCE PROVES THERE ARE ONLY TWO GENDERS*, MALE AND FEMALE (June 2023).

67% OF VOTERS SAY *BIOLOGICAL MALES WHO IDENTIFY AS WOMEN HAVE AN UNFAIR ADVANTAGE OVER BIOLOGICAL FEMALES* WHEN THEY ARE ALLOWED TO COMPETE IN WOMEN'S SPORTS (February 2022).

75% OF VOTERS SAY THAT *CHURCHES SHOULD HAVE THE RIGHT TO REFUSE TO PERFORM SAME-SEX MARRIAGE* CEREMONIES IN ACCORDANCE WITH THEIR BELIEFS (August 2022).

68% OF VOTERS SAY THAT *STUDENTS SHOULD BE ALLOWED TO HOLD BIBLE STUDIES* AND OTHER RELIGIOUS ACTIVITIES IN PUBLIC SCHOOLS (March 2022).

57% OF VOTERS WOULD *RATHER LIVE IN A COMMUNITY WHERE PEOPLE ARE ALLOWED TO OWN GUNS* (May 2022).

76% OF VOTERS AGREE WITH THE FOLLOWING STATEMENT: *LANGUAGE POLICING HAS GONE TOO FAR*; BY AND LARGE, PEOPLE SHOULD BE ABLE TO EXPRESS THEIR VIEWS WITHOUT FEAR OF SANCTION BY EMPLOYER, SCHOOL, INSTITUTION, OR GOVERNMENT. GOOD FAITH SHOULD BE ASSUMED, NOT BAD FAITH (May 2022).

Deep Dive into the Issues

These facts are shaping the reality for everyday Americans, which is why they undergird the motivation for AFPI's commitment to advance policies that put the American people first.

Defend our Constitutional Rights of Religious Liberty and Freedom of Conscience.
- More than 80% of the world's population lives in countries where religious liberty is threatened, restricted, or banned.
- 81% of Americans believe Coach Joe Kennedy should not have been fired for silently praying after football games in Bremerton, Washington.
- 44% of voters think the American legal system is hostile to religious expression.
- 64% would side with their religious beliefs over the government.
- 55% think teachers should be allowed to lead prayer in public schools.

Defend Our Constitutional Right to Keep and Bear Arms.
- 46% of American adults have a gun in their household.
- One in five American households purchased a gun between March 2020 and March 2022.
- In 2022, about 17.4 million guns were sold in the United States. From January 1 to May 31, 2023, an estimated 7.1 million guns were sold, averaging about 1.4 million guns per month.
- More than one in three American adults say that they or someone in their household owns a gun. Of those Americans, 61% say they feel safer because someone in their household owns a gun.
- One-third of gun owners have used a firearm to defend themselves or their property.

Stop Big Tech from Encroaching on Our Free Speech.
- 73% of Americans believe social media sites intentionally censor viewpoints they find objectionable.
- 46% of Americans personally know someone who was temporarily or permanently banned on social media.
- More than 100,000 Americans reported cases of online censorship to AFPI in 2021.
- 65% of Americans believe that people should be able to freely express their views on social media, including views that others find offensive.

Honor the Sanctity of Every Innocent Human Life.
- Six states in the U.S. plus the District of Columbia have no state-level restrictions on when abortion can take place—meaning that fully formed babies can be killed in the womb until the point of birth.

- The U.S. is one of only six countries with laws permitting elective abortions during all nine months of pregnancy, meaning we have more liberal laws than the vast majority of the world. This puts the U.S. in the same group as North Korea, South Korea, China, Canada, and Vietnam.
- Liberals in Congress have attempted to expand radical abortion practices in the entire nation through the "Women's Health Protection Act"—even up to the point of birth—going far beyond *Roe v. Wade* and allowing practices that are indistinguishable from infanticide.
- Three-quarters of Americans believe that "doctors, nurses, or other healthcare professionals who have religious objections to abortion should not be forced to perform them."
- A majority of Americans believe organizations that have religious objections to abortion should not be legally required to provide insurance coverage for abortion.
- 73% of Americans either oppose or strongly oppose using tax dollars to support abortion abroad.

Defend Female Athletes and Preserve Fairness in Women's Sports.
- 64% believe that biological men who identify as women should not be allowed to participate in organized women's sports programs.
- 66% of Americans agree that it should be against the law to perform a sex-change surgery on anyone under the age of 18.

Learn more at: agenda.americafirstpolicy.com/freedom-and-self-governance

4. Give Parents More Control Over Their Children's Education

It has been said that zip codes can determine the outcome of life for many. This is made worse by the decline of public education in the United States because the only option for many children is to attend the public school to which they are assigned. While some schools do well, too many do poorly. Failing schools are not subject to proper accountability, and parents have limited autonomy in choosing the school that would give their children a better chance at a brighter future.

Too many schools are more concerned about which pronouns children should use and about making sexually explicit books available to them than they are teaching them to read and write. For the first time in history, national scores in reading and math fell by the largest margin in more than 30 years. The current school system has failed our children and placed the future of the United States in jeopardy.

A common refrain in recent years has been that we must do certain things for the sake of our children. "Our children," as if the responsibility for kids lies first and foremost with the government or with some faceless collective group. Yet, the Bible makes it clear that it is parents alone who shoulder the responsibility for their children—including supporting their education, building their character, and forging their worldview. Proverbs declares, "Train up a child in the way he should go, and when he is old he will not depart from it." This is a mandate for parents.

Yet many in places of power and influence today would completely usurp the God-ordained role of parents in these vital tasks. The current crisis in public education stems not only from the fact that children are no longer being taught the fundamental subjects and skills necessary to flourish as adults but that they are also being indoctrinated to accept a worldview that is anti-Western, anti-Christian, and, increasingly, anti-reality.

In many places, the current curricula are saturated with radical agendas focused on far-left social experiments, such as gender fluidity, identity politics, critical race theory, and alternative versions of history. The America First Agenda seeks to return education to the oversight of parents, bringing back sound academic principles that restore national unity and pride through a renewed understanding of our founding.

Working to advance educational opportunities for all American families will be a win for our children. The simple, effective solution is to return responsibility for children to parents rather than leaving it to bureaucrats, unions, and politicians. The role of parents cannot be understated in ensuring that children are trained in a Godly manner and set up for a successful life.

KEY SCRIPTURES

"Direct your children onto the right path, and when they are older, they will not leave it."
Proverbs 22:6 (NLT)

"And these words which I command you today shall be in your heart. You shall teach them diligently to your children, and shall talk of them when you sit in your house, when you walk by the way, when you lie down, and when you rise up."
Deuteronomy 6:6–7 (NKJV)

Public Opinion

Below is a list of recent polling data that highlights what the American people think about these issues.

From Scott Rasmussen National Surveys

80% OF VOTERS *FAVOR GIVING PARENTS MORE CONTROL* OVER THE EDUCATION OF THEIR CHILDREN (June 2022).

54% OF VOTERS SAY *SCHOOL CHOICE PROGRAMS PROVIDE BETTER EDUCATIONAL OPPORTUNITIES* FOR STUDENTS (August 2023).

58% OF VOTERS *FAVOR VOUCHER PROGRAMS THAT ALLOW TAX DOLLARS TO FOLLOW CHILDREN* TO THE SCHOOLS OF THEIR PARENT'S CHOICE (August 2023).

76% OF VOTERS *BELIEVE THAT PARENTS SHOULD BE PRIMARILY RESPONSIBLE FOR TEACHING CHILDREN ABOUT SEX* (July 2023).

75% OF VOTERS ARE *CONCERNED ABOUT WHAT CHILDREN ARE BEING TAUGHT* IN SCHOOL THESE DAYS, WITH 43% OF VOTERS FEELING VERY CONCERNED (February 2022).

WHEN GIVEN A CHOICE BETWEEN CANDIDATES, **45%** *OF VOTERS SAY THEY WOULD VOTE FOR THE CANDIDATE WHO WOULD GIVE PARENTS MORE CONTROL OVER WHAT STUDENTS ARE TAUGHT WHILE 38% OF VOTERS SAY THEY WOULD VOTE FOR THE CANDIDATE WHO WOULD GIVE TEACHERS AND OTHER EDUCATION PROFESSIONALS MORE CONTROL* (August 2023).

76% OF VOTERS SAY THAT *SCHOOLS SHOULD NOT TEACH CHILDREN THAT THEY CAN CHANGE THEIR GENDER* (August 2023).

71% OF VOTERS BELIEVE THAT IF A CHILD TELLS HIS OR HER TEACHER OF A DESIRE TO CHANGE GENDER, THE *TEACHER SHOULD BE REQUIRED TO NOTIFY THE PARENTS* (May 2022).

76% OF VOTERS BELIEVE THAT THE *MOST APPROPRIATE WAY TO TEACH U.S. HISTORY IS THAT AMERICA WAS FOUNDED ON THE IDEALS OF FREEDOM, EQUALITY, AND SELF-GOVERNANCE.* THIS INCLUDES TEACHING THAT OUR NATION HAS A TRAGIC HISTORY OF RACIAL INJUSTICE BUT THAT WE HAVE MADE AND CONTINUE TO MAKE PROGRESS (August 2023).

43% OF VOTERS *OPPOSE TEACHING CRITICAL RACE THEORY* (CRT) TO PUBLIC SCHOOL STUDENTS, WITH 30% OF VOTERS *STRONGLY OPPOSING IT* (August 2023).

Deep Dive into the Issues

These facts are shaping the reality for everyday Americans, which is why they undergird the motivation for AFPI's commitment to advance policies that put the American people first.

Give Parents Control by Allowing Them to Select the School Their Child Attends.
- Students who live in states that offer more school choice have higher reading and math test scores.
- Standardized test scores significantly improved for students who exercised school choice compared to similar students who did not exercise such choice.

Give Every Parent the Right to See All Curriculum Materials in Every Class Their Child Attends.
- 84% of voters believe that parents should be able to see all curriculum plans and materials for classes their children take.
- 56% of voters strongly support curriculum transparency.
- 68% of voters believe most public schools have lowered standards rather than demanding more from students.
- 56% of voters believe public school boards do not respect the role of parents.
- 63 parental-rights bills were introduced or pre-filed in 24 states for the 2023 legislative session, and both North Carolina and Iowa enacted laws to increase parents' rights.

Encourage Schools to Teach Basic Skills that Prepare Students for Life as an Adult.
- 45 million borrowers in the U.S. had a total student loan debt of $1.7 trillion as of the first quarter of 2023.
- In a 2018 study, only one-third of adults could answer at least four of five financial literacy questions regarding mortgages, interest rates, inflation, and risk.
- Less than one-quarter of U.S. children ages 6-17 years old exercise for the recommended 60 minutes per day.

Advocate for Teaching the Truth About America's History.
- 80% of Americans oppose using classrooms to promote political activism to students.
- 75% of parents with K-12 students do not believe schools should teach that "the founding ideals of liberty and equality were false when they were written, and America's history must be reframed."
- Nearly 66% of Americans surveyed believe America's public schools are on the wrong track.
- Just 24% of Americans believe schools are headed in the right direction in terms of what children are being taught.
- 69% of Americans oppose schools teaching that America was founded on racism and is structurally racist.

Learn more at: agenda.americafirstpolicy.com/education

Finish the Wall, End Human Trafficking, and Defeat the Drug Cartels

One of the most devastating humanitarian crises that the United States has ever experienced is developing right now at the southern border of the country. Scores of people in search of a better life for themselves and their families in the United States are coming from all over Central America and around the world, but they are illegally crossing our open border. While you can sympathize with those seeking a better life, most migrants are making false asylum claims about fleeing from persecution. This is not honorable and makes a mockery of the immigration system as a whole. God is a God of order and not of chaos, and without a secure border and the restoration of law and order in the area, the crisis will only escalate, and the notorious cartels will continue to take advantage of the vulnerable through drug and human trafficking. Because of the current situation, the border states are no longer just at the border. Every state of the Union has become a border state as the effects of this crisis are felt all over the country.

Without secure borders and coherent control of immigration, the sovereignty of the nation is in jeopardy, and the ability of the government to properly govern and protect citizens is compromised. This is also a catastrophic disservice and categorically unfair to those who are seeking to come to the United States legally, especially those who have legitimate claims to flee persecution from their native country. This is also unfair to those who are seeking to come to the United States legally in pursuit of the American Dream.

The Bible instructs us to both love our neighbor and to consider the plight of the poor. Yet, the effects of open, unprotected borders are devastating to our most vulnerable neighbors and fellow citizens.

Ending the grotesque practice of human trafficking must be among the primary driving motivations to secure the border. Additionally, the millions of poor, unskilled job seekers flooding into our Nation put downward pressure on the wages of the working poor. This is precisely why powerful corporate business interests have lobbied for open borders for decades. Cheap labor further enriches multinational corporations while impoverishing the working class.

These same policies are a gift to known and suspected terrorists and the drug cartels. In the current situation, the United States is importing human misery and death while empowering the dangerous drug cartels that have made our neighbor to the south a hotbed of lawlessness, murder, and human trafficking. Meanwhile, winking at violations of U.S. immigration laws undermines the fundamental commitment to the "rule of law" that holds our society together. The current system has failed. It costs the U.S. taxpayers millions of dollars to run the processing centers that handle the migrants, which are still inefficient.

A country without meaningful, controlled borders is not really a country at all in any basic sense of the term. The America First Agenda seeks to provide greater security for all Americans by securing the border, ending human trafficking, and defeating the Mexican drug cartels.

KEY SCRIPTURES

"Like a city that is broken into and without walls so is a person who has no self-control over his spirit."
Proverbs 25:28 (NASB)

"And then will I declare to them, 'I never knew you; depart from me, you workers of lawlessness.'"
Matthew 7:23 (ESV)

"Rescue those who are being taken away to death; hold back those who are stumbling to the slaughter."
Proverbs 24:11 (ESV)

THE AMERICA FIRST AGENDA

- ★ Finish the Wall
- ★ Stop Human Trafficking by Instituting Effective Border Security and Immigration Enforcement Programs
- ★ Defeat the Drug Cartels
- ★ Modernize and Restore Integrity to the Immigration System
- ★ Boost Counterterrorism Capacity and Defend Critical Infrastructure

Public Opinion

Below is a list of recent polling data that highlights what the American people think about these issues.

From Scott Rasmussen National Surveys

85% OF VOTERS **FAVOR SECURING THE BORDER**, ENDING HUMAN TRAFFICKING, AND DEFEATING THE DRUG CARTELS (June 2022).

68% OF VOTERS **BELIEVE THAT ILLEGAL IMMIGRATION IS BAD FOR THE UNITED STATES**, BUT LEGAL IMMIGRATION IS GOOD (October 2023).

VOTERS RANK **IMMIGRATION AS THE GREATEST THREAT TO AMERICA'S NATIONAL SECURITY** (September 2023).

77% OF VOTERS **BELIEVE IT IS IMPORTANT FOR THE UNITED STATES TO SECURE THE SOUTHERN BORDER** AND END ILLEGAL IMMIGRATION, WITH 51% OF VOTERS BELIEVING IT IS VERY IMPORTANT (June 2023).

73% OF VOTERS **BELIEVE THE TRAFFICKING OF CHILDREN FOR SEX IS A VERY SERIOUS PROBLEM** (July 2023).

48% OF VOTERS **FAVOR BUILDING A WALL TO SECURE THE SOUTHERN BORDER** OF THE UNITED STATES, WITH 30% STRONGLY FAVORING IT (October 2022).

49% OF VOTERS SAY THAT ALLOWING MORE THAN A MILLION PEOPLE TO **ENTER THE COUNTRY ILLEGALLY IS MORE COSTLY TO AMERICAN TAXPAYERS** THAN BUILDING A WALL TO SECURE THE BORDER (October 2022).

60% OF VOTERS CONSIDER THE SURGE OF ILLEGAL IMMIGRANTS ACROSS THE SOUTHERN BORDER TO BE **AN INVASION OF THE UNITED STATES** (September 2023).

BY A **56%** TO **29%** MARGIN, VOTERS OPPOSE REQUIRING ILLEGAL IMMIGRANTS TO REMAIN IN BORDER STATES (September 2023).

67% SAY THAT INDIVIDUAL STATES **SHOULD HAVE THE RIGHT TO DEFEND THEIR OWN BORDERS** IF THE FEDERAL GOVERNMENT FAILS TO DO SO (September 2023).

Deep Dive into the Issues

These facts are shaping the reality for everyday Americans, which is why they undergird the motivation for AFPI's commitment to advance policies that put the American people first.

Finish the Wall.
- 450 miles of new border wall were built between January 2017 and January 2021, and 250-300 more miles were fully funded.
- In one short 12-mile section in the San Diego Sector, the wall reduced U.S. Customs and Border Protection (CBP) manpower needs by 150 agents every 24 hours, saving taxpayers $28 million per year in salaries and benefits.
- In the Yuma Sector, illegal entries in areas with the new border wall system dropped by 87% from fiscal years 2019-2020.
- In the El Paso Sector, drug smuggling efforts fell by as much as 81% in areas with the border wall system.
- Illegal apprehensions at the southern border increased by 278% to 1.7 million in fiscal year 2021 since construction of the border wall was halted.
- Over 1.7 million "gotaways" are estimated to have crossed the southern border since the beginning of the Biden Administration.

Stop Human Trafficking by Instituting Effective Border Security and Immigration Enforcement Policies.
- Cartels engaged in human trafficking and/or smuggling earn as much as $14 million per day by taking advantage of the porous southern border.
- Nearly 500,000 victims of human trafficking are located in the U.S.
- Nearly 71% of all reported incidents of human trafficking were related to sex trafficking.
- A record 2.38 million illegal apprehensions were made along the southern border in FY 2022.
- 150,000 unaccompanied alien children (UACs) entered the U.S. in 2021, an increase of 339% from 2020 figures.

Defeat the Drug Cartels.
- Transnational Criminal Organizations (TCO) and Drug Trafficking Organizations (DTO) represent a clear and present danger to stability in Central America and have widespread secondary and tertiary impacts on the U.S.
- Illegal immigration, which has skyrocketed under the Biden Administration, contributes to the growth and power of TCOs and DTOs.
- Illegal immigration is an integral part of the drug supply chain, as the cartels move illicit drugs into the country while the Border Patrol is preoccupied with apprehending illegal aliens.
- Mexican cartels reportedly earn upwards of $14 million per day for their human smuggling activities.

Modernize and Restore Integrity to the Immigration System.
- The U.S. has more immigrants than any other country in the world, with more than 45 million people having been born in another country.
- The U.S. awards about 1.1 million lawful permanent residents (LPR) with a green card each year. Less than 15% of this total is based on the alien's merit.
- Hundreds of thousands of aliens are in the U.S. on temporary work visas across the economy, with no meaningful labor protections for American workers.

Boost Counterterrorism Capacity and Defend Critical Infrastructure.
- Every day, DHS stops an average of 10 aliens on the terrorist watchlist from entering the U.S.
- Today, nearly 200 joint terrorism task forces exist throughout the nation.
- Cyberattacks using malware spiked 358% in 2020, and cyberattacks using ransomware increased by 435%.

Learn more at: agenda.americafirstpolicy.com/border-security

Deliver Peace Through Strength and American Leadership

America has the greatest potential to lead globally when it places the safety and well-being of Americans first, which can only be done by encouraging a strong military and maintaining peace domestically and abroad. Our military strength should be used first as a deterrent to the adversary. War should always be the last resort for achieving the best interests of the American people. Rev. Billy Graham wrote the following on war and the Christian's perspective: "But war is certainly not the Christian's preference to settle either individual or global problems. War is one of the consequences of living in a fallen world in which sinful men and women are unable to settle differences between each other by peaceful means." A strong military provides the deterrent that will lead to the preservation of peace at home and abroad.

The America First approach recognizes the value of a strong military as a part of strengthening relationships with allies across the globe. Military strength can provide the U.S. a seat at the table with adversaries who only respond to power. Peace through strength promotes relationship-building, global accountability, and the protection of citizens at home. While military power is necessary, it must be coupled with a strong economy. In the modern world, the power of a nation is defined not only by its military might but by its ability to use economic power strategically to promote stability and cooperation that serves the interests of its nation, thus avoiding war and developing economic prosperity. Strong economies foster stability and peace at home and abroad.

Christians should always strive to live at peace with everyone. When conflicts arise and threaten the peace and security of the American people, an armed response must satisfy the principle of a "just war." This means that a war is justifiable for moral or legal reasons, such as a war fought to preserve morality and justice. Peace and security are promised often throughout Scripture. God promises to help the vulnerable and punish those who exploit those weaker than themselves. It is the sacred job of a righteous government to recognize good and evil accurately. The America First Agenda seeks to restore and renew American military strength to protect our people and deter the worst actors in a dangerous world.

Ultimately, peace through strength must be directed toward the good of America and the world. We also know that other powerful nations can be anything but a force for good. The Chinese Communist Party (CCP), for example, oppresses its people (especially Christians), threatens its neighbors, and is guilty of appalling, genocidal human rights abuses. The CCP currently represents the premier national security threat to the United States. China's concerning activities include chronic unfair trade practices, theft of American technologies, aggression against its neighbors, abuse of the environment, and an accelerating nuclear weapons program. Communist China must be held fully accountable.

America must also continue to be a force for good in the Middle East, with three premises: stand with our friends, stand up to our adversaries, and seek new ways to resolve longstanding challenges. In Iran, the U.S. has rejected a deeply flawed nuclear plan that had the wrong ambitions and promoted terrorism. The U.S. should also continue to counter Boycott, Divestment and Sanctions (BDS) falsehoods and rising antisemitism and instead promote Israel-supportive policies. Importantly, America First policies will always stand with Israel.

Around the globe, the U.S. military is depended upon by friends and enemies to be a force of strength and unity in the world. Most importantly, it is tasked with protecting the American people and their freedoms by maintaining peace through military strength and using force when necessary. AFPI seeks to put Americans first in foreign policy decisions and to foster strong, accountable relationships abroad.

KEY SCRIPTURES

"In peace I will both lie down and sleep, for You alone, LORD, have me dwell in safety."
Psalm 4:8 (NASB)

"'Because of the devastation of the poor, because of the groaning of the needy, now I will arise,' says the LORD; 'I will put him in the safety for which he longs.'"
Psalm 12:5 (NASB)

"For rulers are not a terror to good works, but to evil. Do you want to be unafraid of the authority? Do what is good, and you will have praise from the same. For he is God's minister to you for good. But if you do evil, be afraid; for he does not bear the sword in vain; for he is God's minister, an avenger to execute wrath on him who practices evil."
Romans 13:3–4 (NKJV)

"If possible, so far as it depends on you, be at peace with all people."
Romans 12:18 (NASB)

"For the Lord your God is the One who is going with you to fight for you against your enemies, to save you."
Deuteronomy 20:4 (NASB)

Public Opinion

Below is a list of recent polling data that highlights what the American people think about these issues.

From Scott Rasmussen National Surveys

86% OF VOTERS *FAVOR DELIVERING PEACE THROUGH STRENGTH AND AMERICAN LEADERSHIP* (June 2022).

84% OF VOTERS SAY *FOREIGN POLICY IS AN IMPORTANT POLITICAL ISSUE* RIGHT NOW (September 2023).

60% OF VOTERS *FAVOR THE U.S. MILITARY FOCUSING EXCLUSIVELY ON THE MISSION OF PROTECTING OUR NATION*, WITH 25% OF VOTERS STRONGLY FAVORING THIS IDEA (July 2022).

50% OF VOTERS, WHEN GIVEN A CHOICE BETWEEN TWO PRESIDENTIAL CANDIDATES, *SAY THEY WOULD VOTE FOR THE CANDIDATE WHO PROMISED TO SUPPORT AMERICA FIRST POLICIES WHILE ONLY 20% OF VOTERS SAY THEY WOULD VOTE FOR THE CANDIDATE WHO PROMISED TO DEFEND THE LIBERAL WORLD ORDER* (July 2022).

20% OF VOTERS SAY *WAR/INTERNATIONAL CONFLICT IS THE GREATEST THREAT* TO AMERICA'S NATIONAL SECURITY (July 2023).

41% OF VOTERS SAY IT IS POSSIBLE TO *SLOW THE GROWTH OF MILITARY SPENDING* WITHOUT PUTTING OUR NATIONAL SECURITY AT RISK (July 2022).

58% OF VOTERS *BELIEVE AMERICA'S ALLIES TAKE ADVANTAGE OF OUR NATION* AND EXPECT THE U.S. TO PAY MORE THAN OUR FAIR SHARE OF ALLIANCE DEFENSE COSTS (July 2022).

66% OF VOTERS CONSIDER *CHINA AN ENEMY OF DEMOCRACY* (August 2022).

65% OF VOTERS THINK THAT *CHINA IS ACTIVELY TRYING TO REPLACE THE UNITED STATES* AS THE WORLD'S LEADING SUPERPOWER (December 2022).

Deep Dive into the Issues

These facts are shaping the reality for everyday Americans, which is why they undergird the motivation for AFPI's commitment to advance policies that put the American people first.

Establish an America First Foreign Policy.

- An America First approach to foreign policy is based on the idea that America is best positioned to lead in the world and preserve peace and stability when it places the safety, prosperity, and overall well-being of the American people first.
- To be clear, America First does not mean America alone; rather, it offers the surest path to working productively with other nations in a manner that advances Americans' interests and security while avoiding economic overreach and unnecessary military conflicts.
- The Abraham Accords, signed in September 2020, was the first peace agreement between Israel and its neighbors in more than 25 years and the first-ever normalization of relations between the Israelis and the citizens of other Middle Eastern nations.
- After the signing of the Doha Agreement with the Taliban in February 2020 to begin intra-Afghan peace talks, not a single American service member was killed in Afghanistan from that moment until the end of the Trump Administration.

Maintain the World's Most Powerful Military Force.

- The U.S. has spent more than $8 trillion on efforts to fight terrorism across 85 countries.
- Prior to the FY 2023 National Defense Authorization Act (NDAA) striking down the COVID-19 vaccine mandate for our service members, the Biden Administration carried out one of the largest discharges of service members in U.S. history.
- Of note, almost all service members' requests for relief from the vaccination requirement were denied, with denial rates across the service branches of 99.53% for the Air Force, 99.75% for the Army, 100% for the Navy, and 99.83% for the Marine Corps.
- Real (inflation-adjusted) federal government expenditures on national defense increased by more than $100 billion, or roughly 14%, between 2016 and 2020.
- Federal national defense expenditures fell by approximately $80 billion (-10%) between 2008 and 2016.

Pursue a Bold New Path to Peace and Prosperity in the Middle East.
- The Abraham Accords yielded the first joint military exercise between Israel and Gulf states, the first free trade agreement between Israel and the UAE, and other forms of unprecedented cooperation between Israel and its neighbors.
- In 2017, the Palestinian Authorities (PA) paid terrorists and their families $350 million. All U.S. taxpayer dollars going to the PA were halted until it ceased paying families of terrorists.
- To date, 35 states have enacted some form of legislation to counter Boycott, Divestment and Sanctions.

Hold Communist China Fully Accountable for Chronic Unfair Trade Practices, Stealing American Technologies, and Polluting our Planet's Air and Oceans.
- The People's Republic of China (PRC) has the largest army and largest naval fleet in the world.
- As a constant aggressor against the free and democratic island of Taiwan through political, media, and psychological warfare, Beijing's official policy is to "reunify" with Taiwan, including via military invasion if necessary.
- The PRC is rapidly growing its nuclear warhead stockpile.
- The Chinese Communist Party's (CCP) systematic intellectual property theft has cost the U.S. hundreds of billions of dollars.
- COVID-19 originated in Wuhan, China, and has killed nearly one million Americans, crippled our economy, and damaged our supply chains.
- China releases up to one billion tons of plastic waste into the ocean annually.

Learn more at: agenda.americafirstpolicy.com/strengthen-leadership

Make America Energy Independent

God created energy in various forms. In Genesis, He clearly directs mankind to harness the Earth and subdue it. This means humanity must take hold of God's creation and rule over it with responsibility, care, and authority. In other words, mankind is called to stewardship over the natural resources of the world and to use the world's abundant wealth for the betterment of our environment, communities, and society.

The United States is among the cleanest consumers and producers of energy in the world. When compared to other regional powers like China and Russia, the United States continues to lead the way with clean energy. Not only that, but the United States uses its energy power globally to bring further stability to other regions. This is why when politicians speak of things like the "Green New Deal" and other disastrous measures that impact American energy independence, the American people should take note. Measures like these will destroy jobs and cripple the American economy. Scores of jobs depend on American energy and on harnessing the full potential of our energy stores for American economic growth and prosperity.

Sovereign nations are responsible for their natural resources. The care of this wealth is to be stewarded with responsibility and intentionality for the betterment of the whole society and the well-being of American families.

A broad survey of the Bible reveals that God's conception of "good government" or "just rule" is one that advances the well-being of all the citizens of a nation—not just an elite and powerful few. The Scriptures also make it clear that God is the creator of the universe and everything in it and that He delegated dominion and stewardship over the Earth to mankind.

Current energy policy in the U.S. often seems to assume that we have no right to utilize the Earth and its resources for human benefit wisely. At the same time, our policies seem to benefit an elite few in the "green energy" sector while placing additional financial burdens on everyday Americans.

Therefore, the America First Agenda seeks to promote energy policies that wisely steward America's vast energy resources for the benefit of all Her people, not just a few. This agenda is grounded in sound principles of free-market economics and transparent governance with a focus on maintaining a transparent and fair regulatory environment for all energy sources to compete. The agenda also has an emphasis on eliminating harmful regulations and barriers to industrial growth, investing in infrastructure, creating jobs, protecting the environment, and reducing dependence on unstable foreign energy sources. As a sovereign nation, the U.S. should be able to increase its energy independence and allow American ingenuity and strength to flourish. This independence is also healthy due to its support of American jobs and avoidance of potential conflicts with others who could withhold energy resources that we may be depending on for everyday life.

True energy independence means that the U.S. does not fall victim to the whims of energy cartels, adversaries, or unreliable foreign suppliers for its energy needs. When the U.S. is energy independent, the American people enjoy lower-cost energy and insulation from instability around the globe—including the care and security of "the least of these" among us.

Energy independence is at the core of sovereignty. The United States need not be dependent on foreign sources of energy. God has blessed the United States with natural resources, which has led to American leadership in energy production, innovation, and the development of cleaner energy. This innovation should be supported, not restricted by burdensome regulations that stifle the innovative spirit empowered through the Holy Bible and supported by the U.S. Constitution as both issue the responsibility of stewardship to the people.

KEY SCRIPTURES

"Then God blessed them and said, 'Be fruitful and multiply. Fill the earth and govern it. Reign over the fish in the sea, the birds in the sky, and all the animals that scurry along the ground.'"
Genesis 1:28 (NLT)

"[God] doesn't care how great a person may be, and he pays no more attention to the rich than to the poor. He made them all."
Job 34:19 (NLT)

"Moreover, the profit of the land is for all . . ."
Ecclesiastes 5:9 (NKJV)

"For the LORD your God will bless you as he has promised, and you will lend to many nations but will borrow from none. You will rule over many nations, but none will rule over you."
Deuteronomy 15:6 (NIV)

THE AMERICA FIRST AGENDA

★ Become Energy Independent to End America's Reliance on Foreign Sources of Oil and Gas

★ Lower the Price of Gas and Energy by Increasing the Production of America's Energy Supplies

★ Create a Predictable, Transparent, and Efficient Permitting Process and Regulatory Environment

★ Provide Clean Air, Clean Water, and a Clean Environment for All Americans

★ Become an Energy Superpower by Exporting America's Energy Abundance

Public Opinion

Below is a list of recent polling data that highlights what the American people think about these issues.

From Scott Rasmussen National Surveys

87% OF VOTERS **FAVOR MAKING AMERICA ENERGY INDEPENDENT** (June 2022).

84% OF VOTERS SAY **ENERGY INDEPENDENCE IS AN IMPORTANT POLITICAL ISSUE RIGHT NOW** (September 2023).

90% OF VOTERS **AGREE THAT OIL AND NATURAL GAS PRODUCTION PLAYS AN IMPORTANT ROLE** IN STRENGTHENING THE UNITED STATES ECONOMY (June 2023).

86% OF VOTERS THINK IT IS **IMPORTANT TO REDUCE OR ELIMINATE OUR RELIANCE ON FOREIGN SOURCES OF ENERGY,** WITH **57% THINKING IT IS VERY IMPORTANT** (May 2022).

88% OF VOTERS THINK THAT IT IS *IMPORTANT TO PRODUCE NATURAL GAS AND OIL* IN THE UNITED STATES (June 2023).

73% SAY IT IS POSSIBLE FOR THE *U.S. TO GENERATE ALL THE ENERGY* WE NEED HERE IN OUR COUNTRY (May 2022).

67% OF VOTERS *STRONGLY OR SOMEWHAT FAVOR OPENING FOR ENERGY DEVELOPMENT* THE FEDERAL LANDS AND WATERS THAT HAVE SIGNIFICANT ENERGY RESOURCES TO RESTORE AMERICAN ENERGY INDEPENDENCE
(October 2023).

53% OF VOTERS *FAVOR BUILDING NEW NUCLEAR POWER PLANTS* IN THE UNITED STATES (MAY 2022).

62% OF VOTERS ARE *NOT WILLING TO PAY MORE THAN $25 A MONTH* TO REDUCE GREENHOUSE GAS EMISSIONS (July 2023).

40% OF VOTERS THINK THE *BIDEN ADMINISTRATION'S POLICIES MAKE IT HARDER FOR THE UNITED STATES* TO BECOME ENERGY INDEPENDENT WHILE *32% OF VOTERS THINK THAT THE CURRENT ADMINISTRATION'S POLICIES MAKE IT EASIER FOR OUR COUNTRY TO BE ENERGY INDEPENDENT AND 14% OF VOTERS THINK THAT THEY HAVE NO IMPACT* (October 2023).

Deep Dive into the Issues

These facts are shaping the reality for everyday Americans, which is why they undergird the motivation for AFPI's commitment to advance policies that put the American people first.

End Reliance on Foreign Sources of Oil and Gas.
- The U.S. is 100% dependent on imports for 17 critical minerals.
- The U.S. is more than 50% dependent on imports for an additional 29 critical minerals.
- The U.S. imports more than 90% of its uranium from foreign suppliers.
- The U.S. increased nuclear power generation to the highest level on record in 2019 and increased renewable energy production to record levels.
- In 2019, the U.S. became a net energy exporter while also leading the world in CO2 emissions reductions in the same year.

Lower the Price of Gas and Energy by Increasing Production of America's Energy Supplies.
- Low-income households spend, on average, 8.6% of their gross household income on energy, compared to just 3% for non-low-income households.
- Net electricity generation from nuclear power plants is projected to fall by 17% by 2025 or 8% by 2050. This represents a critical loss of clean baseload power generation at the expense of grid reliability and energy affordability.
- Between 2010 and 2025, about 199 gigawatts (GW) of coal-fired electricity generation capacity will have been retired. This will represent a one-third reduction since 2011 and will expose Americans to the risk of diminished grid reliability and larger electricity bills.
- Renewable energy accounted for 70% of the new planned electricity generation capacity in 2021 but currently accounts for only 12% of primary energy consumption.
- Fossil fuels accounted for more than 70% of primary energy production in the U.S. in 2021.
- Wind accounted for just 3% of primary energy production in the U.S. in 2021.

Create a Predictable, Transparent, and Efficient Permitting Process and Regulatory Environment.
- The average environmental impact statement required under NEPA for a single project was more than 600 pages long before reforms under the previous administration.
- A single project previously took agencies an average of 4.5 years to complete.
- The U.S. has not invested in the construction of new refining capacity since the 1970s.
- Refining capacity in the U.S. has been reduced by more than 1 million barrels per day.

Provide Clean Air, Clean Water, and a Clean Environment.
- During the past 30 years, the U.S. has reduced concentrations of criteria air pollutants by more than 77%.
- At the same time, energy production increased by 44%, and the economy grew by more than 350%.
- The combined emissions of the six core pollutants fell by 7% from 2017 to 2019, resulting in cleaner air.
- Energy-related carbon dioxide emissions declined by an estimated 2.9% in 2019—the largest absolute decline in such emissions of any country in the world.
- In 2019, the U.S. became a net energy exporter for the first time in 70 years.

Become an Energy Superpower by Exporting America's Energy Abundance.
- In 2021, the U.S. became the world's leading LNG exporter, experiencing a 1,800% increase since 2016.
- Fossil fuels make up more than 80% of the global energy mix and are projected to remain a dominant player through 2050.
- Two-thirds of America's natural gas reserves are located in the Appalachian region's Utica and Marcellus shale deposits.
- 10% of the world's population lives without access to electricity; nearly half of these are located in sub-Saharan Africa.
- The Biden Administration has doubled the Obama Administration's initial emissions targets. The previous targets have been estimated to cost the U.S. economy 2.7 million jobs by 2025 and as much as 6% of GDP annually by 2030.

Learn more at: https://agenda.americafirstpolicy.com/energy

8 Make It Easy to Vote and Hard to Cheat

Abomination is a strong word, and the Bible uses it sparingly. Yet, the Bible's wisdom book, Proverbs, tells us that "a false balance is an abomination to the Lord" (Proverbs 11:1). Likewise, the Scriptures are full of condemnation for cheating, bribery, injustice, and falsehood.

These truths speak directly to the importance of restoring and preserving integrity and transparency in America's voting and vote-counting processes. No republic or representative democracy can survive long without widespread confidence in the fairness and legitimacy of the electoral process. Without that confidence, our Nation will dissolve further and further into partisan chaos. Our extraordinary Nation will tear itself apart. Every eligible voter should have the opportunity to cast one ballot that is counted once. Anything that fails this simple test is a failure of the system, and the people responsible for that system should be held accountable. One fraudulent vote, or one administrative mistake, is one too many when it comes to protecting each sacred vote. The best election integrity policies make it easy to vote and hard to cheat.

One way of effectively protecting the validity of every vote and voter is the requirement of a government-issued photo ID at the time of voting. Seventy-one percent of Americans support the requirement of a photo ID to prove a person's identity when casting a ballot. A common argument against an ID requirement is that there would be a disproportionate impact on minority populations. However, this argument does not consider the fact that photo IDs are already required to buy alcohol, board a domestic flight, drive a car, and open a bank account—all activities in which the broader public, including minority populations, regularly participate. In fact, twenty-five states have already established requirements for government-issued IDs for the purpose of voting.

Voter rolls should also be accurate, transparent, and cleaned regularly to protect against voter fraud. If an employee joins an organization, that individual must fill out paperwork to be added to the payroll. If the individual leaves the company, the company immediately updates its payroll so that the employee is not improperly compensated. In the same manner, states must proactively keep their voter rolls current and accurate to ensure that we can trust our voting system.

Ensuring ballots are counted accurately and in a timely manner is crucial to making it easy to vote but hard to cheat. We must also advocate for measures that protect the chain of custody for ballots between the time they are cast and the time they are counted. Ballot harvesting is the transportation of ballots to various voting locations by a third party on behalf of a voter or group of voters. This process allows for abuse of the ballot chain of custody and for ballots to be placed in boxes without proper monitoring. States should prioritize transparency and accountability by ensuring that ballot harvesting is not a means by which individuals can cheat and disrupt the integrity of the election process.

In 2020, under the guise of wanting to assist with COVID-19 relief efforts, the Zuckerberg Foundation sent half a billion dollars to local government election entities. State governments promised to use the funds for personal protective equipment (PPE) and voter turnout efforts. However, this private money was instead used by election officials to target certain areas and voter groups. This practice of giving money to election officials to influence an election erodes Americans' confidence in free and fair elections. America First policies must discourage the use of private grant monies to usurp governmental authority and illegally alter our election procedures. This will allow states to maintain proper control over their elections.

The America First Agenda seeks to promote policies that assure every citizen eligible to vote can do so easily and that America's elections, at every level, are transparent, fair, and just.

KEY SCRIPTURES

"You shall do no injustice in judgment, in measurement of length, weight, or volume. You shall have honest scales, honest weights, an honest ephah, and an honest hin: I am the LORD your God, who brought you out of the land of Egypt."
Leviticus 19:35–36 (NKJV)

"False weights and unequal measures—the LORD detests double standards of every kind."
Proverbs 20:10 (NLT)

THE AMERICA FIRST AGENDA

★ Require Voters to Have Photo Identification
★ Clean Up Voter Rolls before Every Election
★ Require All Ballots to be Returned by Election Day
★ Eliminate Ballot Harvesting
★ Ban the Practice of Billionaires Giving Money to Election Officials to Influence an Election

Public Opinion

Below is a list of recent polling data that highlights what the American people think about these issues.

From Scott Rasmussen National Surveys

88% OF VOTERS **FAVOR MAKING IT EASY TO VOTE AND HARD TO CHEAT** (June 2022).

77% OF VOTERS SAY THAT WHEN SOMEONE REGISTERS TO VOTE, THAT PERSON **SHOULD BE REQUIRED TO SHOW PROOF OF CITIZENSHIP** (August 2023).

71% OF VOTERS SAY THAT **REQUIRING EVERYONE TO SHOW A PHOTO ID BEFORE VOTING** MAKES THEM MORE CONFIDENT THAT THE VOTES WILL BE ACCURATELY COUNTED AND THE PROPER WINNERS DECLARED, WITH 41% FEELING MUCH MORE CONFIDENT (July 2022).

68% OF VOTERS SAY **REQUIRING EVERYONE TO SHOW A PHOTO ID BEFORE VOTING** MAKES OUR ELECTIONS FAIRER, WITH 41% SAYING MUCH FAIRER (July 2022).

82% OF VOTERS SAY *A VOTE SHOULD NOT BE COUNTED IF A MAIL-IN BALLOT IS SUBMITTED WITHOUT ANY SIGNATURE* (August 2022).

70% OF VOTERS SAY *A VOTE SHOULD NOT BE COUNTED IF A SIGNATURE ON A MAIL-IN BALLOT DOES NOT MATCH A SIGNATURE* ON FILE (August 2022).

77% OF VOTERS *FAVOR REQUIRING ALL MAIL-IN BALLOTS TO BE RECEIVED BY ELECTION DAY* (November 2022).

74% OF VOTERS SAY THAT DROP BOXES SHOULD BE AVAILABLE ONLY IN PLACES AND TIMES *WHERE THEY CAN BE SUPERVISED* AND HAVE VIDEO SURVEILLANCE (August 2023).

53% OF VOTERS SAY THAT *VOTERS SHOULD BE REQUIRED TO CAST BALLOTS IN THEIR OWN PRECINCTS* (August 2023).

86% OF VOTERS *FAVOR REQUIRING STATES TO CLEAN VOTER ROLLS* BY REMOVING FROM VOTER REGISTRATION LISTS PEOPLE WHO HAVE DIED OR MOVED OUT OF THE RELEVANT JURISDICTION (November 2022).

Deep Dive into the Issues

These facts are shaping the reality for everyday Americans, which is why they undergird the motivation for AFPI's commitment to advance policies that put the American people first.

Require Voters to Have Photo Identification.
- 25 states do not have photo ID requirements to vote, and 15 states with photo ID requirements have a loophole that allows a person who forgets his or her photo ID to cast a ballot without using a photo ID.
- 46 out of 47 European countries require a photo ID to vote.
- Mexico has required all voters to present a photo ID since 1991. Every voter in Mexico must have a tamper-proof photo ID that includes a thumbprint and embossed hologram.

Clean Up Voter Rolls Before Every Election.
- Nearly two-thirds of Colorado's counties had a voter registration rate of more than 100%, making it the most voter fraud-ridden state in the Nation. More than one in six registrations in some Colorado counties belonged to an inactive voter.
- In Michigan, about 26,000 names of deceased individuals were found to be on the voter rolls. About 5,000 of these people had been dead for 20 years.

- Recently, in North Carolina, more than 430,000 names were removed from voter rolls statewide after determining that they were ineligible to vote.
- 92,000 live ballots of active voters in Nevada were returned as undeliverable in 2020.

Require All Ballots to be Returned by Election Day.
- 18 states and the District of Columbia currently allow ballots to be counted after Election Day.
- 32 states require ballots to be received by Election Day.
- The highest grace period for returning ballots is 10 days.
- 43% of voters submitted ballots by mail in the 2020 general elections.
- Just over 23% of voters submitted ballots by mail in the 2016 general elections.
- Voter confidence in the accuracy of the presidential election fell to 59% from 2018 to 2020, a decrease of 11%.

Eliminate Ballot Harvesting.
- According to the National Conference of State Legislatures, nine states allow a family member to submit a ballot in place of a voter.
- 31 states allow the voter to choose someone to submit the ballot in his or her place, although some states have set limits on who can collect the ballots or how many they are allowed to collect.
- Alabama is the only state to require a ballot to be returned by the recipient of the ballot.
- 13 states say nothing about ballot collection, which allows unfettered ballot harvesting.

Ban the Practice of Billionaires Giving Money to Election Officials to Influence an Election.
- $10 million in private money was given to the City of Philadelphia to be used to purchase PPE, but only $225,000, or about 2%, was spent on PPE.
- Election officials in Philadelphia spent almost all of the $10 million on the turnout of targeted voters.
- In Pennsylvania, 92% of Zuckerberg's money was directed to counties whose populations voted for Joe Biden.

Learn more at: agenda.americafirstpolicy.com/election-integrity

Provide Safe and Secure Communities So All Americans Can Live Their Lives in Peace

The Bible declares in Proverbs 29:16: "When the wicked are multiplied, transgression increases; But the righteous will see their fall." This biblical statement and countless examples from history provide a sober warning: When respect for the rule of law disappears, when criminals at every level of society go unpunished, when the law-abiding, productive, and vulnerable live in fear...society unravels. No such nation can remain truly great or even long survive. Also, when law enforcement is portrayed as the villain by mainstream media and is disrespected when enforcing good laws that protect American communities and freedoms, the social contract between society and leaders breaks.

America's greatness sits on a foundation of self-governance and respect for the rule of law. These principles, in turn, find their foundation in Jesus' "Golden Rule"—that is, to treat others the way we would want to be treated (Matthew 7:12, Luke 6:31). This ethic is the glue that has held our society together for more than two centuries. However, many national and local leaders are intentionally, willfully dissolving that vital adhesive by promoting ill-conceived progressive movements attacking law enforcement and allowing crimes to go unpunished. Positions of authority were set in place by God so that a citizen's freedoms could be enjoyed without being threatened by those with ill intent.

However, threats and instability continue to mount. Not only are the schools being filled with intellectual threats from the Chinese Communist Party, but the streets are burdened by the homeless, many of whom are battling mental illness, along with organized crime, such as human trafficking and drug dealing. Furthermore, mobs across the country are conducting coordinated smash-and-grab jobs on respectable businesses, and the police and store owners have very little ability to intervene in these brazen robberies. All American children and adults should be able to thrive in their communities without falling victim to violence, drugs, or other crimes that can destroy their families and their futures.

Security within our communities must also be fostered at home, within the nuclear family. Without a father in the home, children are five times more likely to live in poverty and have higher rates of suicide, develop behavioral disorders, and experience homelessness. Unfortunately, decades of political mismanagement and misaligned incentive structures within our welfare system have exacerbated the problem of fractured families. In response, the local church must rise up and support the family and empower fathers to lead their families with conviction and strength.

As a nation of self-governed individuals and families, we have the privilege (and responsibility) to elect those who value the rule of law and who will ensure that the law is enforced to serve and protect families and communities. This is the very essence of the biblical word "justice." The America First Agenda seeks to restore law and order, restore justice, support law enforcement, and provide secure communities for the safety of ALL Americans.

KEY SCRIPTURES

"I also examined on earth: where the halls of justice were supposed to be, there was lawlessness; and where the righteous were supposed to be, there was lawlessness."
Ecclesiastes 3:16 (ISV)

"For I, the LORD, love justice; I hate robbery…"
Isaiah 61:8 (NIV)

"Let every soul be subject to the governing authorities. For there is no authority except from God, and the authorities that exist are appointed by God."
Romans 13:1 (NKJV)

"Remind the people to be subject to rulers and authorities, to be obedient, to be ready to do whatever is good, to slander no one, to be peaceable and considerate, and always to be gentle toward everyone."
Titus 3:1-2 (NIV)

"The righteous care about justice for the poor, but the wicked have no such concern."
Proverbs 29:7 (NIV)

THE AMERICA FIRST AGENDA

- ★ Restore the Rule of Law
- ★ Promote Respect for Law Enforcement
- ★ Stop Chinese Communist Malign Influence and Theft of American Intellectual Property
- ★ Address Homelessness and Mental Health and the Issues that Plague Our Streets
- ★ Unravel Organized Crime, Human Trafficking Rings, and Drug Trade within Our Cities
- ★ Strengthen Fatherhood and the Nuclear Family
- ★ Create a Pathway to a Second Chance

Public Opinion

Below is a list of recent polling data that highlights what the American people think about these issues.

From Scott Rasmussen National Surveys

90% OF VOTERS **FAVOR PROVIDING SAFE AND SECURE COMMUNITIES** SO THAT ALL AMERICANS CAN LIVE THEIR LIVES IN PEACE (June 2022).

71% OF VOTERS HAVE A **FAVORABLE OPINION OF LOCAL POLICE DEPARTMENTS**, WITH 32% HAVING A VERY FAVORABLE OPINION (August 2022).

42% OF VOTERS WHO HAVE PERSONAL INTERACTIONS WITH POLICE OFFICERS **RATE THEIR PERFORMANCE AS EXCELLENT** (May 2022).

65% OF VOTERS SAY **POLICE OFFICERS IN THEIR AREA HAVE STRONG SUPPORT** FROM THEIR COMMUNITY (May 2022).

81% OF VOTERS AGREE WITH THE FOLLOWING STATEMENT: *POLICE MISCONDUCT AND BRUTALITY AGAINST PEOPLE OF ANY RACE IS WRONG,* AND WE NEED TO REFORM POLICE CONDUCT AND RECRUITMENT. MORE AND BETTER POLICING IS NEEDED FOR PUBLIC SAFETY, AND THAT CANNOT BE PROVIDED BY "DEFUNDING THE POLICE." (May 2022).

ONLY **11%** OF VOTERS SAY *POLICE OFFICERS ARE THE WEAKEST LINK* IN AMERICA'S SYSTEM OF JUSTICE (May 2022).

82% OF VOTERS *BELIEVE IT IS IMPORTANT FOR CHILDREN TO BE RAISED IN A HOUSEHOLD WITH BOTH THEIR MOTHER AND THEIR FATHER PRESENT, WITH 52% BELIEVING IT IS VERY IMPORTANT* (June 2023).

60% OF VOTERS *BELIEVE IT IS THE ROLE OF THE FATHER TO BE THE HEAD OF THE HOUSEHOLD* (June 2023).

54% OF *VOTERS BELIEVE CHILDREN RAISED WITHOUT THEIR FATHER PRESENT ARE AT A SIGNIFICANT DISADVANTAGE* COMPARED TO OTHER CHILDREN (June 2023).

Deep Dive into the Issues

These facts are shaping the reality for everyday Americans, which is why they undergird the motivation for AFPI's commitment to advance policies that put the American people first.

Restore the Rule of Law.
- 12 major cities broke annual homicide rates in 2021.
- In the Nation's major cities, homicides were 42.6% higher in 2022 (9,138 total) compared to 2019 (6,406 total).
- In 2022, robbery increased by 13%, larceny by 20%, motor vehicle thefts by 21%, and residential and nonresidential burglaries by 6% and 8%, respectively.
- After previously cutting the Portland Police Bureau's budget by $16 million, Portland Mayor Ted Wheeler was forced to add millions back to the police budget and offer a $25,000 signing bonus to recruit new officers amid a rising crime wave.

Promote Respect for Law Enforcement.
- Washington, D.C., cut $15 million from the budget for its police department in 2020.
- Washington, D.C., experienced a 15% increase in homicides from 2020 to 2021.
- Ambush attacks on police increased by 115% in 2021.
- 67% of U.S. adults want the police presence in their communities to stay the same.
- 20% of Black Americans and 24% of Hispanic Americans want a greater police presence in their communities.

Stop Chinese Communist Influence and IP Theft.
- Chinese theft of American IP costs between $225 billion and $600 billion annually.
- The 75 Confucius Institutes, 65 of which are on U.S. college campuses, are a threat to our Nation's security and a platform for Chinese Communist intelligence collection.
- 500 Confucius Classrooms are on K-12 campuses throughout the U.S.
- The FBI has arrested dozens of individuals accused of spying on behalf of the PRC while on American soil. These include individuals who worked within the intelligence community and sensitive industries affecting U.S. national and economic security interests.

Address Homelessness and Mental Health Issues in the Streets.
- Unsheltered homelessness increased by more than 50,000 individuals during the last five years.
- Sheltered homelessness has decreased each year since 2014.
- 60% of crimes in Los Angeles involving homeless individuals are violent, compared to 32% of all crimes in the city that are violent.

- Four people die in Los Angeles homeless camps every single day.
- At least three in four unsheltered homeless individuals self-report mental health and substance abuse conditions.
- About eight in 10 voters want their legislators to ban street camping.

Unravel Organized Crime, Human Trafficking, and Drugs.
- Annual drug overdoses in the U.S. exceeded 100,000 in 2021 for the first time ever, making drug overdoses the leading cause of death for young Americans.
- U.S. Customs and Border Protection seized 14,700 pounds of fentanyl at our Nation's ports of entry in FY22. This is enough to kill every American 10 times over.
- Enough fentanyl was caught crossing our border in 2021 to kill 2.54 billion people.
- About 28,100 gangs are active across the U.S., with activity in all 50 states.
- Gang violence accounts for 13% of all homicides and nearly half of all violent crimes.
- Gangs are responsible for facilitating about 85% of all sex trafficking in some areas of the country.

Strengthen Fatherhood and the Nuclear Family.
- 23% of American children are raised in a one-parent home.
- Without a father in the home, children are five times more likely to live in poverty than a child in a married-couple home.
- 90% of all homeless and runaway children come from fatherless homes.
- 63% of teens who commit suicide and 85% of children and teens with behavioral disorders come from fatherless homes.
- 71% of all adolescent patients in drug and alcohol treatment centers come from fatherless homes.
- Children without fathers at home are nine times more likely to drop out of high school.

Create a Pathway to a Second Chance.
- Federal prisons are 60% overcapacity.
- 2 million people are currently in our Nation's prisons and jails—a 500% increase in the last 40 years.
- 90% of people going to prison in America will eventually be leaving.
- About three out of four people remain unemployed a year after being released from incarceration.
- About 70 million U.S. adults have criminal records.

Learn more at: agenda.americafirstpolicy.com/safer-communities

Fight Government Corruption by Draining the Swamp

"Power tends to corrupt, and absolute power corrupts absolutely," warned Britain's Lord Acton. We are told in Proverbs that when godly men and women are in authority, the nation's people rejoice. But when the wicked are in power, the people groan as a result. The presence of corruption in leadership has a lasting impact on a nation's future through how decisions are made in the present.

Here in America, as we have prospered as a nation, our national government has gathered more and more power to itself—far more than our country's founders could have possibly imagined. And with that power has come the temptation to reward friends and cronies at the taxpayers' expense. In recent years, both the cost and reach of the government have soared, and so have the temptations to engage in exploitation, corruption, and bloated inefficiency at every level. Fortunately, it is not too late to reverse course and solve these problems. To "drain the swamp" and restore a government of the people, by the people, and for the people, we must fight government corruption and move federal agencies and decision-making closer to the people. America First policies seek to reform the civil service to create accountability and instill the true tenets of servant leadership throughout the corridors of the federal bureaucracy. The goal is to rid American policymaking of corruption and put the American people first once again.

Putting America first in this area means leading with integrity and honor and serving the people of the country. What the American people are now witnessing is the weaponization of government against political opponents and their supporters. At its core, this weaponization reflects the corruption that has taken root in the bureaucracy, which was originally created to serve the people of this great country. God's people are clearly instructed to pray for leaders and those with governing authority. In a republic, we are also responsible for electing representatives who will serve the people and not undermine the trust of the electorate by pursuing vicious agendas to eliminate political opponents. We are called to submit to the authority of leaders but are never asked by God to go against His Word. The America First Agenda keeps leaders accountable for approaching policy with integrity and righteousness, pursuing policies that not only put the people first but align with the will of God.

To further the America First Agenda, the concentrated and unaccountable government power of the administrative state must be addressed. Congress has delegated some of its powers to other branches of government, resulting in executive agencies doing much of the federal policymaking instead of elected policymakers. The danger of these agencies making decisions on Americans' behalf is that Americans never voted for them. Therefore, these agencies are insulated from oversight by the American people and can wield nearly unrestricted power. Government by the people must be restored.

Americans have the right to self-governance and must hold those in power accountable for upholding the founding documents, keeping a balanced budget, and aligning with the people's priorities, not those of bureaucrats. As God has instituted positions of authority, Americans are called to pray for those in power—that they will align their vision with that of the Lord. When a nation's God is the Lord, we know that the nation will experience the blessings of God. The America First Agenda seeks to promote policies and outcomes that restore integrity, efficiency, transparency, and accountability to our institutions.

KEY SCRIPTURES

"When the godly are in authority, the people rejoice. But when the wicked are in power, they groan."
Proverbs 29:2 (NLT)

"While they promise them liberty, they themselves are slaves of corruption…"
2 Peter 2:19 (KJV)

"Without wise leadership, a nation falls; there is safety in having many advisers."
Proverbs 11:14 (NLT)

"Woe to the sinful nation, a people whose guilt is great, a brood of evildoers, children given to corruption! They have forsaken the LORD; they have spurned the Holy One of Israel and turned their backs on him."
Isaiah 1:4 (NIV)

"Have nothing to do with the fruitless deeds of darkness but rather expose them."
Ephesians 5:11 (NIV)

"Do not pervert justice or show partiality. Do not accept a bribe, for a bribe blinds the eyes of the wise and twists the words of the innocent."
Deuteronomy 19:19 (NIV)

Public Opinion

Below is a list of recent polling data that highlights what the American people think about these issues.

From Scott Rasmussen National Surveys

86% OF VOTERS **FAVOR FIGHTING GOVERNMENT CORRUPTION AND DRAINING THE SWAMP** (June 2022).

72% OF VOTERS **BELIEVE IT IS VERY IMPORTANT TO RESTORE PUBLIC TRUST IN THE FEDERAL GOVERNMENT** (July 2022).

51% OF VOTERS **BELIEVE THE FEDERAL GOVERNMENT TODAY IS A THREAT TO THE FREEDOM** AND LIBERTY OF INDIVIDUAL AMERICANS (September 2023).

63% OF **VOTERS HAVE AN UNFAVORABLE OPINION OF MEMBERS OF CONGRESS** (September 2023).

39% OF VOTERS TRUST THAT THE *FEDERAL GOVERNMENT WILL DO THE RIGHT THING ONLY SOME OF THE TIME* (July 2022).

57% OF VOTERS *BELIEVE THAT THE UNITED STATES PROVIDES TOO MUCH GOVERNMENT CONTROL*, WITH 27% BELIEVING IT PROVIDES FAR TOO MUCH CONTROL (September 2023).

41% OF VOTERS SAY THAT THE *PRESIDENT OF THE UNITED STATES HAS TOO MUCH CONTROL OVER THE AGENCIES* OF THE FEDERAL GOVERNMENT (July 2022).

57% OF VOTERS THINK THAT THE 50,000 SENIOR GOVERNMENT *OFFICIALS PURSUE THEIR OWN POLICY AGENDA* IN POLICY DECISIONS INSTEAD OF SERVING THE AMERICAN PEOPLE (July 2022).

67% OF VOTERS *BELIEVE THE GOVERNMENT SHOULD BE MORE RESPONSIVE TO VOTERS* AND SHOW LESS DEFERENCE TO POLICY EXPERTS TO RESTORE TRUST IN THE FEDERAL GOVERNMENT (July 2022).

67% OF VOTERS *BELIEVE CUTTING THE GROWTH OF GOVERNMENT SPENDING WOULD BE BEST FOR THE U.S. ECONOMY, WITH 37% BELIEVING IT SHOULD BE CUT BY MORE THAN 1%* (September 2023).

Deep Dive into the Issues

These facts are shaping the reality for everyday Americans, which is why they undergird the motivation for AFPI's commitment to advance policies that put the American people first.

Fight Government Corruption.
- 14 Members of Congress were convicted of criminal offenses between 2012 and 2022.
- Over the past three years, at least 78 Members of Congress violated the STOCK Act, a law intended to combat insider trading by Members of Congress.
- Federal ethics rules generally prohibit senior executive branch officials from owning more than $15,000 worth of individual stocks. These ethics rules do not apply to Members of Congress or their staff members.
- Executive branch agencies fulfilled more than 838,000 FOIA requests in FY 2021. Congress did not fulfill any FOIA requests because FOIA does not apply to Congress.

Move Federal Agencies Closer to the People.
- Federal employees enjoy 17% higher salary and benefits than comparable private sector workers.
- 283,000 federal employees work in the Washington, D.C., metropolitan area.
- The Washington, D.C., metropolitan area contains five of the seven wealthiest counties or county-equivalents in the U.S.:
  — *Loudon County, Virginia (median household income of $147,100)*
  — *Falls Church City, Virginia (median household income of $146,900)*
  — *Fairfax County, Virginia (median household income of $127,900)*
  — *Howard County, Maryland (median household income of $124,000)*
  — *Arlington County, Virginia (median household income of $122,600).*
- The Washington, D.C., metropolitan area has the fifth-highest cost of living out of 267 urban areas in the U.S.
- Cost-of-living arrangements raise federal salaries in the Washington metropolitan area to 13% higher than what federal employees earn in the rest of the U.S.
- Relocating 100,000 federal jobs from the Washington, D.C., metropolitan area to the rest of the U.S. would save taxpayers $1.4 billion per year in federal employee locality pay adjustments.

Cut the Red Tape.
- Federal agencies reduced net regulatory costs by $199 billion during the four years of the Trump Administration.
- The Council of Economic Advisors estimated that the Trump Administration's deregulatory reforms would raise annual household incomes by $3,100 a year once they took full effect.
- Federal agencies increased net regulatory costs by $201 billion in 2021, the first year of the Biden Administration.
- Americans will take an estimated 131 million hours to complete the paperwork created by new regulations finalized in 2021.

Reform the Civil Service.
- Non-veteran federal employees were first given removal appeals in 1962.
- It now takes an estimated six to 12 months for federal agencies to dismiss a poor performer. This figure does not include subsequent appeals.
- Just 26% of federal supervisors are confident they could remove a demonstrated poor performer.
- Only one-third of federal employees report that their agency takes steps "to deal with a poor performer who cannot or will not improve."
- Fewer than 4,000 out of 1.6 million tenured federal employees were dismissed for poor performance or misconduct in 2020.
- 58% of Americans believe it is too hard to fire poorly performing government employees.
- State employees in Arizona, Georgia, Missouri, and Texas serve at will as do managers and supervisors in the Florida state government.
- Agencies spend $200 million annually to subsidize federal union operations.

Dismantle the Administrative State.
- The U.S. federal government has 278 executive branch departments, bureaus, agencies, and sub-agencies.
- The Biden Administration issued 3,273 final rules, including 164 "significant" final rules, during President Biden's first year in office. Elected Members of Congress did not vote to approve any of these rules, but they legally bind the American people.
- 55% of voters believe letting government bureaucrats set rules without approval from Congress or voters is a major threat to democracy.
- Only 25% of the Department of Health and Human Services rules were issued by officials appointed by the president and confirmed by the United States Senate. Many of these rules were instead issued by career bureaucrats.
- 28 independent agencies are led by officials whom the president cannot remove at will. These independent agencies include the National Labor Relations Board, the Federal Trade Commission, and the Federal Energy Regulatory Commission.
- 1,931 administrative law judges (ALJs) and 10,831 non-ALJ executive branch employees perform quasi-judicial adjudications in the executive branch.

Balance the Budget.
- Federal outlays are projected to total $6.2 trillion in 2023, or 23.7 percent of GDP, according to the Congressional Budget Office (CBO).
- CBO estimates deficits will increase from 5.3 percent of GDP in 2023 to 6.9 percent of GDP in 2033.
- Interest on the federal debt acts as a self-reinforcing driver of deficits, with the CBO estimating interest costs to triple from the actual $475 billion in 2022 to $1.429 trillion by 2033.
- The federal government does not have a revenue problem; it has a spending problem. Federal spending growth would need to slow significantly to balance the budget within 10 years.

Learn more at: agenda.americafirstpolicy.com/fight-corruption

AMERICA FIRST AGENDA
In Action

It's Time to Awaken

"You are the salt of the earth; but if the salt loses its flavor, how shall it be seasoned? It is then good for nothing but to be thrown out and trampled underfoot by men. You are the light of the world. A city that is set on a hill cannot be hidden. Nor do they light a lamp and put it under a basket, but on a lampstand, and it gives light to all who are in the house. Let your light so shine before men, that they may see your good works and glorify your Father in heaven."

MATTHEW 5:13–16

For more information, ask for the *America First Agenda: Guide to the Issues*

Want to learn more and support the America First Agenda?

Visit **agenda.americafirstpolicy.com** or scan the QR code.

BIBLICAL FOUNDATIONS
AMERICA FIRST POLICY INSTITUTE

Center for American Values

The core of American government is, as the Declaration of Independence states, "to secure these rights," namely, "life, liberty, and the pursuit of happiness." Today, a dizzying array of ideas and influences counter to foundational American Values threaten our inalienable rights and our democratic republic system of government. The America First Policy Institute's Center for American Values will advance messaging, policies, and litigation that respect and protect life, uphold God-given liberties, preserve freedoms of expression, and restore basic ideals and values that propel a prosperous society. In the same vein, the Center for American Values also features the "Second Chances Project," which aims to address America's incarceration problem through a faith-based lens and confront the root causes of crime: broken families and a lack of faith.

PAULA WHITE-CAIN
CHAIR, CENTER FOR AMERICAN VALUES

DR. RICHARD ROGERS
NATIONAL DIRECTOR OF FAITH ENGAGEMENT & SENIOR FELLOW, CENTER FOR AMERICAN VALUES

Paula White-Cain was born in Tupelo, Mississippi, and serves as the Chair of the Center for American Values at AFPI. Currently, White-Cain serves as Senior Pastor at City of Destiny. For the past 37 years, White-Cain has worked across the world in almost 200 countries, ministering, fighting for religious freedom and humanitarian rights, and advocating for the voiceless. White-Cain also served as an advisor to President Donald J. Trump in the Office of Public Liaison's Faith and Opportunity Initiative.

Dr. Richard Rogers is from Flowery Branch, Georgia and serves AFPI as National Director of Faith Engagement and Senior Fellow, Center for American Values. He earned his doctorate from Pepperdine University. Dr. Rich is currently on Free Chapel College's executive team and has served as the president for the last five years. In addition to his many roles at Free Chapel, he also served as a professor at Pepperdine University for over 20 years. During the Trump administration, he regularly met with faith directors from various departments and agencies.

Access the digital works cited page: